The Story of Deddington

The Story of Deddington

Mary Vane Turner

with an introduction by
Christopher Day

Deddington Map Group
for
Deddington & District History Society
2008

First published in Great Britain by the
Deddington Women's Institute, 1933

This edition published by
Deddington Map Group

ISBN 978-0-9538362-1-5

Produced by
The Deddington & District History Society
℅ Stonecourt
Earls Lane
Deddington
Oxon OX15 0TJ

© 2008

history@deddington.net
www.deddington.org.uk/ddhs

Printed by the MPG Books Group in the UK

INTRODUCTION

Mary Vane Turner's *The Story of Deddington* was published in 1933. It has long been out of print and is presently unobtainable anywhere outside libraries, a recent global internet search having failed to unearth a single copy for sale. The Deddington and District History Society, The Deddington and District History Society, encouraged by Colin Cohen, editor of the Society's newsletter *224*, is therefore marking the occasion of the 75th anniversary of the book's publication by producing a reprint. Colin Cohen and Jill Adams (also a member of the society's committee) have carried out extensive research into Mary Vane Turner's personal history and into the history of the Oxfordshire Federation of Women's Institute Histories series of which *The Story of Deddington* forms part. As a result of their work we now know much more (though by no means everything) about both the author and the series.

This introduction will attempt in part to set *The Story of Deddington* in context as a piece of local historical writing. As Vane Turner notes in her foreword, 'short historical notes' concerning Deddington had been compiled by Rev Edward Marshall and published in 1879 in the *Transactions of the North Oxfordshire Archaeological Society* (the society continues today as part of the Oxfordshire Architectural and Historical Society). The prolific local historian William Wing of Steeple Aston published *A Supplement to Marshall's Deddington* in the NOAS *Transactions* in the same year. Neither Marshall's nor Wing's work has the range or variety of Vane Turner's, and it she who deserves the accolade of publishing the parish's first history.

It should be remembered that there was in the late 1920s and early 1930s relatively little in the way of a tradition of carefully researched and soundly written parish history to which Vane Turner might look as a model. County history had a vigourous and enthusiastic tradition from the Tudor period, though it has to be said that Oxfordshire had less to offer in that regard than many other counties.[1] There were few models when it came to writing a parish history. Nevertheless, Oxfordshire can at least claim the first parish history ever published. White Kennett's *History of Ambros-*

den appeared in 1695. He began research in order to settle a dispute over parochial charities and found historical research absorbing more and more of his time. He felt that he might have achieved more if his research had been better structured, noting disarmingly that 'I often read much to very little purpose', a sentiment that might be echoed by any of us. In fact, the wide range of his sources, his fastidiousness in citing them and his avoidance of baseless speculation (characteristics he doubtless learned while a pupil of the great Oxford antiquary Anthony Wood) made his a work worthy of emulation. North Oxfordshire can claim another pioneering parish history in Thomas Warton's *History of Kiddington* (1785). Warton was not only the incumbent of the parish of Kiddington but at various times Camden Professor of History at Oxford University and Poet Laureate. *Kiddington* was remarkable especially for its deployment of scholarly footnotes and for an awareness of what we would now call landscape history.[2] Otherwise, there was the work of John Dunkin who in 1816 published *The History and Antiquities of Bicester* and in 1823 *The History and Antiquities of the Hundreds of Bullingdon and Ploughley*. Dunkin bequeathed some twenty volumes of his collected material, much relating to North Oxfordshire, to the Bodleian Library in Oxford, where it can still be consulted.[3] Perhaps more pertinently, Vane Turner was able to draw on a tradition of local history developed by women writers from a non-academic background. Of especial note in this regard were Mrs Bryan (Mary Anne) Stapleton's important work *Three Oxfordshire Parishes: a History of Kidlington, Yarnton, and Begbroke*,[4] and Mary Sturge Henderson's *Three Centuries in North Oxfordshire* (1902).

Scholarly women began in the late nineteenth and earlier twentieth century to make an ever greater impact as historians, as editors and as archivists. It would be too much to argue a leadership role for Vane Turner in that emerging army but she was a foot-soldier with a part to play in the advance.[5]

We have no way of knowing to what extent Mary Vane Turner was aware of her role models. Certainly she knew the work of Marshall and Wing, and she refers also to the collections of T A Manchip (former headmaster of

Deddington School), Thomas Smith, and especially Henry Stilgoe, member of a long-established Deddington family and a Fellow of the Society of Antiquaries. Stilgoe's collection of deeds, notes and photographs was clearly a mainstay of Vane Turner's work.[6] It seems very likely that she knew the work of Stapleton and Henderson.

The absence of reliable models was not the greatest obstacle to producing a well-researched history. Deddington, like many places in this part of the world, is well documented, with daunting quantities of archival material in the National Archives, in the Oxfordshire and Northamptonshire County Record Offices, in the British Library, in the Bodleian Library, and in Oxford college archives. But little of this material would have been readily available, if at all, to Vane Turner. The National Archives (then the Public Record Office), the British and Bodleian Libraries, and college archives were unwelcoming to the amateur researcher and their collections were difficult to access and use. The topographical volumes of the *Victoria County History*, whose copious footnotes have often provided researchers with an introduction to sources, had yet to appear for Oxfordshire. The Oxfordshire Record Society series began only in 1919. The Oxfordshire County Record Office did not open until 1936, three years after the publication of *The Story of Deddington*. One begins to appreciate and sympathise with the difficulties facing our author.[7]

The immediate pretext for *The Story of Deddington* was a decision in 1932 of the Oxfordshire Federation of Women's Institutes to encourage local Women's Institutes to produce village histories or, failing that, village books (which were to be historical collections rather than analysis). The single greatest influence was probably the redoubtable Joan Wake of Delapré Abbey, founder of the Northamptonshire Record Society, Northamptonshire county archivist, and author of *How to Compile a History and Present Day Record of Village Life* (1924, for the Northants Federation of Women's Institutes).[8]

The Story of Deddington has in many ways been superseded when looked at as a work of history. Howard Colvin's *A History of Deddington, Oxfordshire*[9] was written for the *Victoria County History* in 1960, but since the Deddington volume was not due to appear for some years a way was found of publishing it 'in advance'. Deddington was fortunate in its historian. Colvin's book is succinct and authoritative, especially strong on earlier history (he was originally a medievalist) and on Deddington's buildings, as one would expect of one of the greatest architectural historians this country has produced. His *History* was revised and expanded by Alan Crossley for *Victoria County History of Oxfordshire* Vol XI, which appeared in 1983.[10] Deddington therefore has good modern professional histories with which we can compare Mary Vane Turner's *Story of Deddington*. There are inevitably a number of errors and omissions in her book. In particular it is somewhat surprising that she seems to have been unaware of the importance of the Cartwright family of Aynho, owners of one of the three manors and of a great deal of property in Deddington. She perpetuates the misconception that the ill-fated Piers Gaveston was held captive during the night of 11-12 June 1312 in Deddington Castle, rather than in Castle House. One could go on, but it is invidious and unfair to highlight them, and they are in any case relatively few.

Arguably the importance of Mary Vane Turner's work, and the chief reason for re-issuing it, is that it has become in its own right a significant historical source. Colvin, Crossley and others since have made extensive use of it. To cite but one example, we should know next to nothing of the Pavilion in the castle grounds, and of its startlingly glamorous role in the social life of the District, without her account, based on excellent oral history. The only photograph of the building known to survive gives the appearance of a reconstructed (and regrettably graffiti-strewn) Iron-Age hut! She is similarly excellent on such diverse topics as the provision of mains services, the Deddington Mummers, the involvement of Deddington men in the Great War, and house history of her period. It is interesting to note the frequency with which Colvin and Crossley (who, remember, had the advantage of access to a range of sources unavailable and even inconceivable to Turner) cite her as a source. In re-issuing her book we are, therefore, making available an important source for the history of Deddington in the later nineteenth and earlier twentieth centuries. That much of her information was based on oral evidence obtained from Deddingtonians long since departed makes it all the more precious.

Despite Mary Vane Turner's modest disclaimer in her Foreword, the *Story* is more than a mere compilation of material, an undifferentiated and uninterpreted collection in the old antiquarian sense. She does, it is true, reproduce some documents and extracts without offering analysis or context, but there is good history, too, as in her account of some Deddington trades on pp 42-43. That said, her account could probably be bettered today, if only because of the greater number of sources and techniques for analysis that are available to us. What we could not replace is the material for which she and her contemporaries are our only source. In that sense she has amply fulfilled her hope that she has supplied 'a link between the more remote past dealt with by others and the present day'.[11] She also has a modest and praiseworthy place, surely to her posthumous surprise, in the ever-evolving line of succession from anecdote and antiquarianism to present-day history and on to lines of research as yet unthought-of.

THE STORY OF *The Story*

The Women's Institute, which originated in Canada in 1897, expanded to the United Kingdom in 1915.[12] A Deddington branch was established in 1925, affiliated to the Oxfordshire Federation.[13] The Women's Institute nationally was keen to promote local history projects, and it was perhaps in response to that lead that in May 1932 the Federation decided to hold a competition for what were termed 'village histories' and 'village books'.[14] Village histories 'need not be long and can contain anything of interest in the village history'. The terms of reference for village books make an interesting period piece and are worth quoting: they were intended 'in the first place for those villages who have nobody with the time for research in old documents and also those who feel they have no history, or whose history has already been published by someone else. The book should have a good many illustrations and fairly long descriptions with as much history as is known. It should have old stories, old customs, old superstitions and remedies, memories of the village which the old people were told in their childhood and modern events as well.'[15] The lack of a similar detailed description of what should be in a village history presumably reflects a misplaced faith in a common assumption about what 'history' comprises. One result was that some entries could equally have been submitted in either category.

In September the original, unrealistic, submission date of December 1932 was sensibly postponed until June 1933.[16] The histories and books 'must be compiled co-operatively and may be written co-operatively'. There were to be for the village histories a first prize of £5 and a second of £3. For the village books there were prizes of £4, £2 and, should there be more than twelve entries, a third prize of £1. Dr R N Marett was asked to adjudicate between the histories and a 'Miss Sidgwick' was asked to judge the village books. Robert Marett (d 1943), an anthropologist, was Rector of Exeter College, Oxford. Miss Sidgwick was possibly Margie Sidgwick, daughter of Arthur and Charlotte. Arthur Sidgwick, of Corpus Christi College, Oxford, was a leading supporter of women's higher education and of women's suffrage. Margie read modern history as a home student at Oxford and it may have been she who secured the services as judge of Dr Marett. In the event he seems to have judged the histories and the books, perhaps because there were fewer entries than hoped-for.

Mary Vane Turner's typescript of *The Story* survives[17] and has, pasted inside the front cover, a copy letter from Robert Marett to the Oxfordshire WI announcing that in the village history section he placed the entry from Shipton-under-Wychwood first. 'Headington Quarry, Deddington and Churchill I bracket as all extremely good and only a little behind the first in interest and general quality of exposition and thoroughness'. There followed the entries from Brize Norton and Chinnor. In a postscript he noted that since a second prize had to be awarded to one entry, he would award it to Headington Quarry. The Shipton entry was written principally by Muriel Groves, of the well-known Wychwood firm of builders of that name. She headed her piece a 'Traditional history'. It does indeed rely on the usual elements, but they were well done. In fact all the entries were resolutely traditional. They typically emphasise old charters, accounts of the manorial lordship, the parish church and its incumbents (though little on nonconformity, with the understandable exception of Headington Quarry where to ignore nonconformity would be simply perverse), and charities. But there was an interesting awareness of and interest in the topographical development of settlement and landscape study, and oral history. Amateur history has a track record of promoting such areas of interest in advance of the professional historian.

It may be a little late to call for a recount, but we in Deddington cannot resist this opportunity of pointing out that the history sections of the Headington Quarry entry were written by no less than E A Greening Lamborn, a prominent local historian and considerable architectural historian and, more to the point, a man.[18]

The entries were returned to their authors in July. At the same time, Miss Sidgwick was to be consulted about 'making an Oxfordshire book'.[19] It was an interesting idea that presumably never came to fruition.[20] If so, the scheme merits a place in the long list of such unfulfilled ventures dating back almost two centuries. But it was an idea whose time had come, to materialise between the stately red and gold covers of the *Victoria County History*.

MARY VANE TURNER[21]

Mary Turner was born Florence Mary Hodges in 1867 in Ealing. Her father Henry was in the insurance business. In 1890 Mary married Hugh Turner. Hugh had matriculated as a Non-Collegiate student at Oxford University in 1878, later migrating to Exeter College, from where he graduated in 1881.[22] He spent some time at Lincoln's Inn before becoming a schoolmaster and subsequently a land agent and secretary of a land company. Mary seems to have adopted her husband's second forename, Vane, and was known during her lifetime as Mary Vane Turner. She is recorded as living at Ilbury House in New Street, Deddington, by 1926.[23] By the later 1930s she lived at Beeches, in Earl's Lane.[24] Her husband had died in 1933.[25] They had two children. Leonard was killed in action 21 December 1914.[26] Muriel (*d* 1936) and her husband Dr George Horatio Jones (*d* 1939) lived in Deddington.[27] Mary died in a Banbury nursing home in 1947 having outlived her husband and both her children.[28]

Muriel's obituary[29] records that she had been responsible for establishing the Deddington WI, whose first President she was. Meetings were held at the British Legion Club, although on at least one occasion Ilbury House was used.[30] Mary became its President in 1933.[31] Occasional references to Mary in the 1930s and 1940s relate chiefly to her charitable activities. A favourite seems to have been The Waifs and Strays Society, a Church of England charity now better known as The Children's Society. Her name occurs regularly in connexion with the parish church, of which she was a generous benefactor. The family no longer lives in Deddington but in 2008 a great-granddaughter, Josephine, and great-grandson, Timothy, live in Gozo and Australia respectively.[32] The family name can be found commemorated in stained glass of high quality in the parish church of St Peter and St Paul. At the east end of the north aisle are two windows whose glass was provided by Dr Jones. The east window is dedicated to his first wife Emily (*d* 1923), that on the north-east to his second wife, Muriel. Both windows were designed by the notable Arts and Crafts artist Archibald Davies of the Bromsgrove Guild.[33]

Chris Day
Deddington, November 2008

1 For an account of local historical writing in Oxfordshire see A Crossley, 'Oxfordshire', in *ed* C R J Currie and C P Lewis, *English County Histories*, p 322-35.
2 Crossley, 'Oxfordshire', p 330.
3 Bodleian MSS Dep d 71-82; *ibid* MS Eng d 2102.
4 Oxford Hist. Soc. Vol. 24 (1893).
5 See J Thirsk, 'Women Local and Family Historians' in *ed* D Hey, *Oxford Companion to Local and Family History*, p 498-504.
6 M Vane Turner, *Story of Deddington*, p 4.
7 For an overview of local historical sources that are now available see W B Stephens, *Sources for English Local History* (Manchester Univ. Press, p 19)
8 Thirsk, *op cit* 503.
9 Published by SPCK (London), 1963.
10 Oxford University Press for London Univ. Institute of Historical Research.
11 *The Story of Deddington*, p 4.
12 History of the Women's Institute at www.thewi.org.uk.

13 Inf. from Virginia Lawrence, Secretary of Oxfordshire Federation WI; *The Story of Deddington*, p 80.
14 Minutes of 19 May 1932: copy kindly made available by Virginia Lawrence.
15 National Federation of WIs, *Home and Country*, Oxfordshire Supplement (March 1933, p 1).
16 Minutes of 21 September 1932.
17 Kindly made available by Betty Hill.
18 The results are recorded in *Home and Country*, Oxfordshire Supplement (28 June 1933, p 328).
19 *Ibid* p 330.
20 *The New Oxfordshire Village Book*, published by the Oxfordshire Federation in 1990, seems to be unrelated to the 1933 publications.
21 What follows draws heavily on the research of Jill Adams.
22 J Foster, *Alumni Oxonienses 1715-1886*.
23 Electoral roll, 1926.
24 *Kelly's Oxfordshire Directory* (1939).
25 Information from Jill Adams.
26 Tomb of Leonard Turner in Perivale Cemetery.
27 Information from Jill Adams.
28 Obituary in *Deddington Deanery Magazine*, August 1947. The nursing home, then known as Madora, was in 2008 No 72 Oxford Road, Banbury.
29 *Deddington Deanery Magazine*, June 1936, p 6.
30 *Banbury Guardian*, Sept. 1932; *ibid* August 1933.
31 *Ibid* 1933, *passim*.
32 We would like to record our gratitude to Josephine for the photograph of Mary, and for giving of her time and knowledge.
33 For a full account of the windows see Elizabeth Tothill, *The Jones Memorial Windows* (Priv. print. Deddington, c 1997)

FOREWORD TO THE 2008 EDITION

Had it not been for Maree Aspinall of Queensland, Australia, who in the spring wrote to Banbury Museum looking for information on her husband's great-grandfather John Clark, we would never have thought of reprinting this book. Her enquiry set me looking for copies of *The Story of Deddington* and I was astonished that although there were a number of copies to be found locally none were to be found for sale on the internet; not even in 'the world's largest collection of unsold books'.

It was then that I started investigating the practicability of reprinting it for the tenth anniversary of the Deddington & District History Society, and the 75th anniversary of its original publication. Having established that it was a viable proposition and would not be beyond the Society's resources we realised that next to nothing was known about the author, Mary Vane Turner. There followed research at the Bodleian Library, the WI's national archive at the Women's Library of London Metropolitan University and at the Oxfordshire Federation of WIs headquarters at Tackley and above all by Jill Adams who has used her great family-history research skills which led to the author's great-grand-daughter and to the portrait of the author which been used on the back cover.

Just as we were about to go to press Buffy Heywood discovered that the author's original typescript and the original photos (those in the printed book were proving a challenge to reproduce) survived along with several other photographs that Mary Vane Turner apparently wanted to include. Only the photos of two paintings of the church interior do not seem to survive, neither have we been able to trace the paintings themselves, so that these have had to be reproduced from the printed book. The captions in the typescript have more detail than in the 1933 printed edition, so we have incorporated this in the new edition.

I am most grateful to Deddington's naturalist, Walter Meagher, who kindly supplied a commentary on Miss Helen Loveday's 'List of Birds in the District' which has been included on the final page of the book, following the index.

I am also grateful to Jeremy Gibson for the loan of a copy of the book in its original binding; to Betty Hill for the loan of the original typescript and photos; to Virginia Lawrence of the OFWI for allowing access to Oxfordshire WI records; to Stella O'Neill, Deddington Library Manager, for the prolonged loan of a copy of the book; to Norman Stone of the Deddington Map Group and many others for technical assistance with aspects of publication and of course to Jo Warren for providing scans of the portrait of her great-grandmother and of the birds-eye view of Deddington and to Jane Hodges.

Colin Cohen, Editor

The Story of Deddington

by

MARY VANE TURNER.

BRACKLEY—NORTHANTS:
J. SMART & CO.,
PRINTERS AND PUBLISHERS,
1933.

**Dedicated
to my daughter,
Muriel Jones.
Our First President.**

Note : This Village History was written for a competition held by the Oxfordshire Federation of Women's Institutes. Dr. Marrett, Rector of Exeter College, Oxford, the Judge, awarded First prize to Shipton-under-Wychwood, Second prize to Headington Quarry, Deddington and Churchill he bracketed together with Quarry as "all extremely good and only a little behind the first in interest and general quality."

CONTENTS.

1. Old Deddington.
2. The Parish Church.
3. Streets and Houses.
4. Trades and Callings.
5. Deddington Folk (Parts I and II).
6. Deddington Fairs.
7. Inns and Coaching Days.
8. Sports and Pastimes.
9. Milestones.

✤

LIST OF ILLUSTRATIONS.
Between pages 64 and 65

1. Bird's Eye Map of Deddington.
2. Stone Effigy in Church.
3. Interior of Church (East End).
4. Interior of Church (West End).
5. Castle House.
6. Nathaniel Stilgoe.
7. The Pavilion.
8. John Knibbs.

✤

APPENDIX.

I. List of Clergy from Early Times.
II. Measurements of Church and Weight of Bells.
III. Armorial Glass in Church (1574).
IV. Old Deed relating to Deddington (1607).
V. Deed relating to the Dissolution of the Guild of the Holy Trinity (1635).
VI. Will of Anthony Stilgoe (1606).
VII. Extracts from Diary of the Rev. W. Cotton Risley.
VIII. List of Field Names.
IX. List of Birds in the Locality.

FOREWORD.

Dear Deddingtonians and Fellow Institute Members,

In presenting to you this story of our village, I make no claim to original research. Already short historical notes had been written—the Rev. E. Marshall's Deddington (issued in the Transactions of the North Oxfordshire Archaeological Society, 1879) and Mr. William Wing's Supplement to the same, are the best known. Mr. T. A. Manchip (late headmaster of Deddington School) and Mr. Thomas Smith had also added much historical and local lore to such facts as Mr. Marshall's scholarship had accumulated. But these records are far from being accessible to the general villager, and even the printed pamphlets of Marshall and Wing are becoming rare. My intention is that ultimately, in some simple form, what I have been able to gather my be easily obtainable to pass from hand to hand to be added to in their turn.

My efforts, however, especially concerning the more ancient past, would have been the merest adaptation—I doubt indeed if the dry bones of history would have stirred at all—had it not been for the help of Mr. Henry Edward Stilgoe, C.B.E., F.S.A., the distinguished Chief Engineer to the Metropolitan Water Board, whose family has been identified with Deddington for many centuries. The loan of old Deeds ; the gift of photographs for illustration ; above all, access to the immensely valuable and interesting notes he has collected about the place and people ; the latter source of information, indeed, forms the life and soul of this narrative in any fresh historical sense. Beyond incorporating in it such knowledge as was already gathered, my own ambition was humble but it was clear. I aimed at supplying a link between the more remote past dealt with by others, and the present day. In this respect I have been fortunate, for our oldest inhabitant, William Hirons, a centenarian who died early this year, lived to impart to me a great deal that would otherwise have been lost. Others, too, with clear recollections of the last half century and longer have kindly helped me, in addition to aid from our Women's Institute.

Thanks are due to the Vicar, the Rev. Maurice Frost, for his photography of often difficult prints, etc., for lending books and for help in searching parish registers and so on. Mr. T. Smith has also been most kind with loans of photographs, books and cuttings, and with many a helpful interview.

If, dear Deddingtonians, this story makes the old life hum again for you as for me, it will bring home this meaning too. The old bygone folk lit the torch of progress, which we hold for a little while and then pass on. If it is to burn brightly in our generation we must work for the realisation of those words of Blake, which the Women's Institutes have adopted as their hymn—not to rest till we have built Jerusalem (the new Jerusalem) 'in England's green and pleasant land.'
Deddington.

November, 1932.

1. OLD DEDDINGTON.

Deddington is set on a hill and cannot be hid. Its market place is 416ft. above sea level, and the measurement to the top of the church tower battlements adds 86½ft. more. No wonder that the parish church of Saint Peter and Saint Paul with its crown of vane-topped pinnacles appears on guard at every approach.

But long before there was a church that summit with its outcrop of hard ribbed ironstone must have been a notable landmark, lifting itself above the misty valleys of Swere and Cherwell. Altitude was valuable for security, and early settlers may well have planned here a strong place not very different from Ilbury Camp, though presenting no such actual traces of fortification. That well-known stronghold of the ancient people is described by the Rev. E. Marshall in his Historical and Descriptive Notes as designed to protect them and their cattle and their perishable dwelling huts within an enclosure defended by natural steepness, earth embankments and felled trees. Mr. Marshall writes of these that "the race was brave, and endowed with capabilities that awaited development"; and there is no reason to doubt that this tribute would not apply to the inhabitants here. In due course opportunity came, a civilisation perhaps first dimly begun through the proximity of a traders' trackway, believed to have existed along the Cherwell Valley from a remote age.

Deddington is on the rock, Clifton in the Clay, with southward the geological stratum called the great oolite. I am privileged to live in a Deddington cottage built of the same stone as the rocky outcrop—a ferruginous marlstone quarried nearby—which shines richly gold in the sunshine. Standing on its threshold I can put my hand on fan-shaped shells, white, with lines delicately etched, embedded in the rough-hewn building blocks. All about, in every golden brown stone wall, even in the slabs of paving, Deddington bears such witness to Earth's strange vicissitudes and unfathomable past. After all modernity merely means 'now', and against a background of much the same mystery and wonder primitive man's sense of the present was vivid as our own. Flint implements are still found in this neighbourhood testifying to an industry and enthusiasm in the artificer comparable to those efforts which have harnessed electricity and are conquering the air.

Here, man looked up, beheld the heavenly bodies and worshipped. Remnants of his faith and rites survive in our superstitions and in many of the things we do. Cards are dealt and wine is passed 'sun wise'; the new moon has great significance for us, is often curtseyed to. We are proud of our dancing county of Oxford, little recking that in the hand-linked circles folk-lorists trace sun-worship, and in those figures danced backs to centre the grim ritual of human sacrifice—victim in the middle, those assisting encircling the altar with averted faces.

....

'The address of this village is Deddington, Oxford', says the Post Office notice. But it was not always a village, it was a Market Town. Now it is accurately a 'decayed Market Town.' It was also a Parliamentary Borough. It is in the Hundred of Wootton and the Union of Woodstock.

Here are some spellings of Deddington. The first carries with it history of origin. It is Daedintun in the signature of Brightuuinus de Daedintun, a witness to an early Charter, A.D.1049-52. The name, Mr. Marshall writes, 'implies that it was the town of the Daedings, the descendant of a settler, or owner, who is designated in the first syllable of the word ; the suffix "tun" denoting the inclosures which had been formed from the open land, or waste, the nucleus of the present town. The name of Clifton is significative of a similar inclosure on the hill-side......while Hempton may be taken as a variation from Hampton, and descriptive of the site of a home or hamlet made by inclosure.' Cliftone, Hamptone, Heentone and Hampton are all found in the ancient spellings. Tabulated, with sources of quotation, the old variations of Deddington run thus :—

A.D.1049-52. Daedintun : Codex Diplomaticus Aevi Sasconici.
    1083-86. Dadintone : Domesday Book.
    1154-63. Dedinton : Cartulary of the Abbey of Eynsham.
    1216-1307. Dadditon : Testa de Nevill Sive.
    1233. Dadynton : Close Rolls of the reign of Henry III.
    1270. Dadinthone : Cartulary of the Abbey of Eynsham.
    1289. Tadynton : Cartulary of the Abbey of Eynsham.
    1312. Dathintone : Geoffrey de Baker's account of the captivity of Piers Gaveston.
    1528. Dadyngton : Lease from Windsor Manor.
    1535. Dodyngton : Grant of Coat of Arms to Thomas Pope of D., Esqre.
    1606. Dadington : Will of Anthony Stilgoe.
    1644. Dedington : Visit of Charles I. (Diary of Capt. Symonds).

Now we always spell it Deddington, but often call it Ded'n'ton.

In Domesday Book, that remarkable monument of surveying, the land here is reckoned among the possessions of Odo, Bishop of Bayeux, half-brother of William the Conqueror, and is thus described :—

"The same bishop holds Dadintone : there are thirty-six hides there : there is land to thirty ploughs : there were eleven hides in the demesne besides inland : there are now eighteen hides and a half in the demesne, and there are ten ploughs there : and twenty-five serfs and sixtyfour villeins with ten bordars have twenty ploughs : there are three mills of fortyone shillings and one hundred eels : and there are one hundred and forty acres of meadow and thirty acres of pasture : from meadows ten shillings : it was worth in King Edward's time and after forty pounds ; now sixty pounds : five thanes."

The King Edward referred to was, of course, the Anglo-Saxon King Edward the Confessor.

Explanation of the terms used cannot be more clearly described than in the words of Mr. Marshall. "Demesne" and "Inland" alike imply the immediate occupation of the lord, who cultivated it by means of those whose services he could compel. But the latter was taken in for culture with the demesne while the former was originally held.

'Of the persons mentioned the "serfs" were the lowest class, and most completely in the power of the lord ; the "villeins" were dependants who were not free, but obliged to certain fixed services ; the "bordars" were cottagers, who also had to perform compulsory services......while the "thanes" were in a social position similar to that of the "knights" of a later period. The rent service of eels was one that was very commonly rendered where there was water.'

The "hide" was not then a fixed quantity, but Mr. Marshall calculates that a measurement of one hundred and six acres to the hide would make it correspond to the area described with an excess of only two acres. It was fixed in the reign of Henry II as consisting of one hundred acres.

OUR THREE MANORS.

That 'the manorial rights of Deddington have from an early period had a threefold division, by which as many separate manors have been formed,' is the statement with which the Rev. E. Marshall heads his chapter number two of learned historical and genealogical research, tracing their origin, inheritance, or creation. The Manors, as every good Deddingtonian knows, are the Duchy Manor, the Windsor Manor and the Christ Church Manor.

The first has a claim to romance for it might be called 'the Dower of Queens', and was the estate of the sovereign in Deddington, now forming part of the Duchy of Lancaster. Royal interest in the Manor began when William de Bohun died in 1360, seised of one-third part, which descended through his son

Humphrey to the latter's two daughters, Eleanor and Mary, who were co-heiresses. Eleanor, the elder, married Thomas of Woodstock, Duke of Gloucester, the youngest son of Edward III, who at his death was entitled to one-third of the Manor of Deddington in right of his wife. Mary, the younger sister, married Henry IV in 1384 and was mother of Henry V., who made provision for the union of his inheritance from her with the Duchy of Lancaster in 1414. In 1420, on the death of Joanna, widow of Humphrey de Bohun, her grand-daughter (daughter of Eleanor, Duchess of Gloucester) Anne, Countess of Stafford became co-heir with Henry V. A partition was made between them, by which the aforenamed portion of the Manor of Deddington, value £13.6.8., came into possession of the king. Then it was assigned by him, and confirmed by Parliament as part of the dower of Catherine de Valois, who was married to him the same year (1420).

The next queen to be so endowed was Margaret of Anjou, queen of Henry VI., and the course of making this portion of the Manor part of the Queen's dower was followed when Edward IV married Elizabeth Gray. The confirmation in the last case was some years after marriage, and took place in 1468. In 1477, by an exchange, this part of the Manor of Deddington became vested in the de la Pole family, but Edmund de la Pole, Duke of Suffolk, conveyed his interest to Henry VII, and the Manor again became vested in the king. The revenues are paid into the Privy Purse as part of the Duchy of Lancaster.

The following extract from the Drapers Hall, Coventry, Muniment Room, (1345), the 18th year of Edward the third's reign) has reference to a queen, Isabella, the king's mother, though the endowment is in respect of another Manor, that of Cheylesmore, near Coventry. The point of interest to us is that it is witnessed among others, by Robertus de Dadyngton "Cancellario meo", (my chancellor).

The Manor of Windsor comprises the Rectorial Estate. By its assignment in 1351, by William de Bohun, patron of our Church, to "the free chapel of St. George the Martyr, situate in the castle of Windsor," (later so designated in the section of an Act of the first of Edward VI protecting it), the integrity of the property was assured and remains to this day.

But more than the patron's act was required, the concurrence of the Pope, the licence of the Crown, and the consent of the bishop (then Lincoln) were necessary. The appropriation of the church to the royal chapel was finally authorized by a Bull obtained from Pope Clement VI which is duly entered at the date of the ordination of the Vicarage, 1352-3, in the register of the then

Bishop of Lincoln. By this appropriation the Dean and Canons of Windsor are enabled to sever the tithes from the incumbency. At first this took place without a fixed stipend for the vicar, but this evil was done away with by the passing of the Acts of the fifteenth of Richard II and the fourth of Henry IV and an independent position in the parish and fixed remuneration secured. The Dean and Canons of Windsor have accordingly for the past close on 600 years appointed our vicars.

The Manor of Christ Church, being the interest possessed by the Dean and Chapter of Christ Church, Oxford, in the third portion of our Manorial distribution, was formerly the estate belonging to the Priory of Bicester. This was originally the donation of Philip Basset, whose uncle, Gilbert Basset, had founded the Priory—the gift is recognised in the abstract of the earlier Rolls of the Hundreds in 1272, as one-third part of this Manor. By an Act (1536) of Henry VIII dissolving all religious bodies with revenues less than £200 per annum, the Priory of Bicester coming under this category, it was granted to Sir Thomas Pope by the king, as 'the Manor of Deddington, late of the monastery of Bicester.' In 1545, it was again in the possession of the king, having been purchased by him of our illustrious Sir Thomas, who rose to such great eminence under that monarch. Subsequently it was conveyed to the Cathedral of Christ Church, as "the Manor of Deddington, late of Sir Thomas Pope, in the king's hand by purchase.'

The legal estate of both Windsor and Christ Church Manors has become vested in the Ecclesiastical Commissioners of England and Wales.

New College, Oxford, were once landlords in a small way in Hempton. The Warden of New College (1879) gave Mr. Marshall an account of that College's property in Hempton, which used to consist of about 50 acres. This has now been exchanged for lands elsewhere with the Dean and Chapter of Christ Church.

THE CASTLE.

Save the captivity of Piers Gaveston, favourite of Edward II, within its walls prior to his execution at Warwick, 1312, no event is recorded which relieves the obscurity in which Deddington Castle is wrapped.

Some names occur in its first mentions, which relate to the early owners of the soil here after the conquest, and to the founder of the Priory of Bicester. 'In 1204' (the fifth of King John), we read in Marshall's Notes, 'Guy de Dyve had seisin (in the nature of a freehold) of Deddington from the king, with the exception of the Castle, which the king retained in his own hands. In the following year, however.........Thomas Basset was directed to deliver the Castle to him (Guy de Dyve) with all the lands of which he had been disseised. Thomas Basset had granted the Manor to his daughter Alice, on her marriage with Walter Malet, Baron of Cury.'

On account of his espousing the cause of the barons against King John, it was forfeited in 1215, the year of Magna Charta, and reverted to the king. 'Upon this', continues Mr. Marshall, 'it was regranted to Thomas Basset, but some interest appears to have remained with his daughter, for in 1229 she conveyed a portion of the land held by her in Deddington to her nephew Gilbert, the son of her brother Alan.

In the following year, the lands of Warine Fitzgerold, in consequence of a similar forfeiture, were granted to Robert Mauduit and Alan de Bocland, who in the year had obtained the Castle and certain land from Guy de Dyve.'

Mr. Marshall's investigations revealed a shuttlecock history of the Castle during the earlier quarter of the thirteenth century as it passed to and fro between its different owners. Dr. Plot, writing in 1676, says that he meets with nothing concerning it till the reign of Edward II. But Kennet found earlier mention that 'the Manor of Deddington had in the tenth of Richard I (1199, the last of his reign) a Castle fortified in it, which soon after belonged to Wida de Diva, whose possessions King John seized, and in the sixth of his reign sent a precept to the Sheriff of Oxfordshire to restore without delay all his lands and chattels, except the Castle of Deddington which the King would keep in his own hands.' The de Dyve family had a long connection with Deddington, the relation ceasing about 1327-8. (Marshall's Notes).

Brewer, the historian, describing the building from personal observation of its still traceable extent writes:—'Deddington possessed a Castle, which from the amplitude of its site was probably a structure of much strength and consequence. No part of the building is now remaining. A wide fosse went completely round and is still distinctly marked through its whole progress, though in some places overgrown......Some persons were digging for building materials at the eastern end of the area......and it appears that the walls in this direction were about six foot thick and had an outward and inner casing of very good stone, the space between being filled with sand and rubble stone. The whole area perhaps comprehended six acres.'

The period of erection cannot be ascertained, but tradition connects it with the Saxon Heptarchy, even surmising it may have belonged to King Alfred's daughter, Ethelfled, 'the Lady of Mercia' (Mercia was the midland kingdom) who was famed as a Castle builder. To give further colour to this theory of Saxon origin, it may be here related than Mr. Duffel Faulkner, the Deddington antiquarian, discovered a coin of the still earlier Offa in the foundations within the grounds.

Piers Gaveston's imprisonment could hardly have been elsewhere than in the Castle, for most certainly he stopped with his captors in this town on that fatal journey to Warwick. Remarking that 'as he has a place in history' only this single incident connecting him with Deddington need be described, Mr. Marshall recalls that having been twice banished the realm, Gaveston re-appeared in 1312, when the opposition to his favourite caused Edward II to place him for security in Scarborough. 'This was besieged by the Earls of Surrey and Pembroke, and Gaveston was forced to surrender, though with a promise of safety, which had been exacted from the Earl of Pembroke by the king. On this condition he was conducted by the earl on the way to his castle at Wallingford, and what followed may be told in the words of a writer from the north of Oxfordshire, Geoffrey le Baker, of Swinbrook......'

"But envy, a principal temptation to fidelity, and a desire to gratify the enemies of Peter (Piers), seduced his custodian, in spite of his oath, into a neglect of vigilance ; and so at last, however much against his will, Peter was brought within the power of his enemies by means of an unfriendly companion. He is taken, that is to say to Dathintone Manor, a place between Oxford and Warwick, where no natural hiding place, nor any castle or stronghold made by art, could conceal him from the near presence of the Earl of Warwick. The Earl of Pembroke retired from Peter by night, and at early dawn the Earl of Warwick arrived with a small number of attendants and with hue and cry. He carried Peter to Warwick Castle......'

Gaveston was beheaded on June 19th, 1312, at a short distance from the castle of Warwick at Blacklow Hill, where a monument marks the exact place of execution. It is said that he had offended the swarthy Earl of Warwick by calling him the "Black Dog,', and that the earl had retorted "the witch's son should feel the black dog's teeth." The captive, as an additional humiliation, is reputed to have been made to ride a mule when setting forth from Deddington Castle at dawn.

The Castle is situate in Windsor Manor and is supposed to have been demolished before the reign of Henry the eighth.

After the Piers Gaveston incident, until the Civil Wars, no high light of history touches our past. Only the records show how manors and lands changed hands, with here and there details of tolls and tithes and rents of mills and farms—smaller transactions between inhabitants striking sometimes a note more intimate. Or there are reprimands and penalties administered by magisterial authority, revealing delinquencies and unfortunate domesticities. Such is the note following, taken from the Calendar of Close Rolls, 5th year of Edward III (1331).

Feb. 2. Langley. 'Peter Perpount acknowledges that he owes to William de Newport Parson of the Church of Dadyngton 160 1. ; to be levied, in default of payment, of his lands and chattels in Co. Essex.'

Or this, published in the report for 1930 of the Oxfordshire Archaeological Society, headed 'Deddington' and heard in the Church there, 9th October, 1540.

'Thomas Barton had a child by Joan Ellys, now dead ; and at the time of her death she said that he was the father of the child. On 11 October he appeared at Chippingnorton and denied it. The judge appointed that he should purge himself with three of his neighbours in the church of St. Martin the next Wednesday. Afterwards he confessed the charge and submitted himself to correction. The judge bid him head the procession on two Sundays with a candle, etc.'

Another paragraph from the same source—'James Brooke has frequented and still frequents the company of the wife of Richard Perkins, in spite of many monitions from his neighbours, etc.,' is quoted in full in part II of the chapter on 'Deddington Folk', as the name of Richard Stilgoe, whom he produced with Thomas Brown at Chippingnorton 'when he took oath (Oct. 11th., 1540) and purged himself,' is the earliest mention hereabouts of a family (the Stilgoes) later and continuously for more than three and a half centuries closely identified with the fortunes of Deddington.

It is noteworthy that the appearance of delinquents in Deddington Church, as head of the Deanery, was followed at an interval of two days by their appearance before the judge at Chipping Norton.

Deddington for a short time enjoyed the privilege of sending two members to Parliament. Here is the note on the subject by the Rev. E. Marshall.

'The burgesses of Deddington were summoned to Parliament by writ in the 30th year of Edward I, 1302, and in the year 32-3, 1304-5. In the former instance the members returned were Robert de Elseffield and Henry Durnall ; and in the latter, John Tankrevy and William Gyllot. There does not appear to be any record of an earlier nor of a later representation, and after this date the borough was disused.'

Looking back we shall not be far wrong in imagining the Deddingtonians of those days accepting as a matter of course their lot of rough toil and hardship—made hardy by it where fair play allowed them to benefit by good harvests. And for gaiety, behold, holy church ever following fast with feast, each season having its own plays and pageants. Failure of crops meant famine, unless extraordinary precautions were observed ; then it meant a scarcity that wore the populace to skin and bone. Transition in industry or agriculture is ever fraught with difficulties for those practising them. Even a change for good is resented for this reason. The coming of England's wool supremacy was an agony to those whose sole vision of plenty lay in golden grain.

The following passage from John Buchan's novel 'the Blanket of the Dark' brings this vividly home. Deddington readers, by the way, will notice that the Oxford writer gives his hero, Peter Bohun, a surname familiar in our annals, William de Bohun having (as already stated) presented the advowson of our parish church to St. George's, Windsor, in January 1351.

Peter Bohun is looking at 'a great wool convoy coming towards him from the Cherwell. He watched the laden horses struggle up the slope, eleven of them, each like a monstrous slug buried in its wool pack......Peter viewed the convoy with no friendly eye. The wool barons were devouring the country side and ousting the peasants. Up in Cotswold the Crevels and Celys and Midwinters might spend their wealth in setting up proud churches, but God would not be bribed.'

By Elizabeth no more raw wool was allowed to be exported, and in consequence the looms of Banbury got busy, a few shuttles flying even in Deddington ; England famous for wool also became famous for cloth. The weavers of Banbury, noted for fanatical piety, are lampooned as 'hanging a cat on a Monday for killing a mouse on a Sunday.' That neighbouring town was industrial centre and storm centre too. Some of the products of its extremist opinions came this way in 1649, when a party of Levellers quartered themselves in Deddington. As the name implies they sought to level all ranks—not a new idea then or now.

Banbury also sent us a noted Puritan Divine, the Rev. Samuel Wells, inducted as its Vicar by order of the House of Lords on September 13th, 1648, but banished under the Five Mile Act at the Restoration, having refused to take the Oath of Supremacy. He abode at Deddington as being outside the prescribed area.

The Civil War raged fiercely round Deddington which was one of the outposts of a region made famous by battles. It was after the battle of Cropredy Bridge that Charles I slept here ; he 'lay at the Parsonage house'—of which event more later. An engagement serious enough to be called the battle of Deddington took place in 1643. But by this period the registers of the parish church, available from 1631, are to hand ; beside usual entries of baptisms, marriages and burials, they throw many an interesting sidelight on the history of the times. The written word is, however, a part only of that national book which lies open for reading, sermons in all its stones—an old English parochial church.

2. THE PARISH CHURCH.

The parish church, dedicated to St. Peter and St. Paul, is built of stone quarried in the neighbourhood, thus fulfilling the law decreeing that fabric should be native to the soil. History of its origin is proclaimed by the name of 'church pits', which quarries were in a field off Paper Mill Lane. There was talk lately of re-opening them, but the idea was abandoned. There are still, however, to be seen huge blocks of this very hard ironstone—less golden that that used generally in Deddington, which is akin to sandstone—lying about the old workings. Here and there, in houses near the church, some of this hard-wearing building material may be discerned, notably in the walls of Tucker's Stores, late the Post Office, long ago an inn, kept it is rumoured by one Kempster, whose family name is closely identified with the parish church in the reign of Charles I and during the first fifteen years of the Restoration.

So obeying the rule of harmony the tower while serving as a landmark blends truly with the countryside, over which its bells peal, the curfew sounding each night at eight. But neither this tower nor those bells are the originals. For the first church tower fell in the year 1635 (O.S.1634) bringing the bells down with it, this mighty crash doing great damage. The story of how all was made good again being told later, it suffices here to remark that the old materials were used in reconstruction, so the very stones consecrated for that early church are those sacred now.

What the first parish church was like can only be surmised from the foundations and earliest parts yet existing. These date from the 13th century, perhaps before. From documentary evidence it is known that Ethelmar de Valence was instituted rector in 1247. He was half brother to Henry III, and his career is a flagant instance of royal favour elevating the undeserving. After obtaining much valuable preferment in the church, he was by King Henry's desire claimant to the bishopric of Winchester, but a petition against his election was presented to the Pope. Ultimately, however, Ethelmar visiting Rome gained the Papal consent to his consecration, despite the fact that a new Bishop had been already elected. Journeying with much pomp to claim his bishopric, Ethelmar only reached Paris to die on December 5th, 1260. His body was buried in the church of Genevieve there, but his heart was brought to Winchester at his own request and placed in the Cathedral, where against the wall, by the side of the Chapel of the Guardian Angels, there is a much disfigured effigy appearing to represent a bishop holding a heart-shaped stone with the words (in Latin) : "To Thee my heart, O Lord."

Before the name of Ethelmar de Valence, one other—Ranulph Brito or Le Bret, Rector, died in 1247—is given in the Rev. E. Marshall's list. These first clergy are indeed names only to us except where a contemporary record makes a man step out of the shadows. Such is the William de Neuport (instituted 1328, died 1332) referred to in the previous chapter, who, we must believe, must have been rich for he was owed the very large sum in those days of one hundred and sixty pounds. And Mr. Manchip in his Notes quotes from the Autographs in the Office of Arms (Beesley's, Banbury) a Quit Claim of Baldwin Piggot (Lord) to the Prior and Canons of Wroxton respecting the advowson of the Church of Onnesby, which is dated 1306. Among the witnesses is 'Sir Hugh, Rector of Dadyngton', this being evidently Hugh de Neuton, rector, who died in 1345. So, if the dates be correct, his rectorship was very long. It is interesting to note the prefix 'Sir' being already customary for the clergy. It did not disappear even at the Reformation, for Shakespeare's parsons are 'Sir'—as, for example, Sir Oliver Max-text in 'As you Like it' ; Sir Nathaniel (a curate) in 'Love's Labour Lost', and Sir Hugh Evans, the Welsh parson of 'The Merry Wives of Windsor.'

There is an interval in Deddington's list of clergy between 1345 and 1523, which Mr. Marshall explains is due to the cessation of Rectors on the appropriation of the church by the Dean and Canons of Windsor. From 1523 thenceforward they were Vicars. This gap roughly marks also a period of transition in the building. Exactly when it is impossible to tell, but somewhere in the century left blank between, the roof's elevation was increased and the clerestory, or clear story, with its six windows a side, added in the wise taste of the 15th century which approved more height and more light.

We must learn what we can of the way of the first architects and masons from the hard stone, beginning with the outside. In the main it is reckoned that the original church including the tower that fell, was 'Decorated', that is in the style which prevailed in the 14th century, which included the latter part of Edward the first's reign and the reign of Henry the fourth. Walking round the chancel exterior the great east window is seen by the pointedness of its high arches to approximate to the 13th century 'Early English' form, though it must be in the main classed as 'Decorated'. Low down on the chancel's south side a small square-topped, blocked-up window calls for attention. This appears to have been used to communicate between the outside and inside of the building and that has led to its being sometimes described as a leper's window. Two recessed arches of the early period are interesting, and where the old south porch formerly opened (the present south porch is a modern addition by Street, the Victorian architect who carried out various restorations) there are traces remaining of the parvise, or priest's chamber, in the thickness of its wall.

One writer after noting that the chancel is comparatively narrow in a building remarkable otherwise for breadth, observes that the church 'follows the usual plan.' This is somewhat vague for there are several well-known plans about which much has been written. But without recourse to expert learning it is obvious that the simplest and oldest of designs has been followed here—that of the ship, dear to all of seafaring habit. Not churches only, but other buildings of importance and permanence were first made like ships turned upside down. The derivation of the word 'nave' is from the Latin 'navis' (a ship) while the German for nave of a church is simply 'Schiff', (ship).

Entering five or six hundred years back, before the clerestory was added, it would have been hard at first to discern much besides the radiance of the sanctuary and other oil-fed lamps, and the scintillation of candles and tapers (all of the best beeswax !) beside which the daylight from those fewer windows would seem blurred. Then, as the vision cleared, details would show ; colouring on the plastered walls (vestiges of carmine remain at the end of the north aisle), and the rood-lofts or screens. Two flights of steps in the north and south aisles, now to be seen each approaching a window, evidently led up to the rood-screens or lofts, which were like elongated platforms, traversing part of the church and furnished with chapels or chantries at one or both ends. These have been surmised by an authority on ecclesiastical architecture to have extended from each side at right angles, almost forming squares, but leaving the nave free. Only the rood screen, specially designed to display the Holy Rood, or Cross, erect or suspended, stretched in front of the chancel, right across from north to south.

Allusion has been made to the recessed arches in the outer wall. One of these in the south aisle contains a stone figure, recumbent in an attitude of prayer. For long there was no clue to its identity, but research seems to establish the fact that it is the effigy of a judge. In the Deddington Deanery Magazine for July, 1931, Mr. F. E. Howard ascribes the effigy to Ralph de Beresford who owned land at Barford St. John in 1315, and was appointed Judge 'itinerant' in 1329. Enquiries made of the Bristol and Gloucestershire Archaeological Society resulted in their recording that John de Stonore, Chief Baron of the Exchequer (1329) buried in Dorchester Abbey (Oxon) is represented in the same coif, tippet, sleeveless gown and long undergarment, thus giving further evidence that the robes are those of a judge, not of a woman or priest as some have declared. The last information is in the September

1931 number of the Deddington Deanery Magazine. The deep crack or cut traversing the robe has been attributed by one antiquarian to the sharpening of 'Round Head' swords therein !

Last, not least, our most ancient and best preserved feature of the 13th century is the Lancet opening, now walled up, which is an Early English doorway and led to the parvise (priest's room) above the original south porch. The hinges of the door remain and two of the flight of steps by which the parson reached his quaint retreat.

Before passing to more spacious days of history—and the church—note should be taken of a brass half-effigy, now affixed to the right-hand side of the Lady Chapel, but as shown in a watercolour drawing of J. Wilkins (a local artist of last century), formerly on the paving midway down the centre aisle. This is labelled "a civilian, circ. 1370." It was noticed in the *Gentleman's Magazine*, vol. LXV., in the year 1795, when a sketch of it was published. In the following number another communication stated "that the figure was not remarkable, representing some burgess, or member of the staple, (wool staple) in the fifteenth century." But in the *Manual of Monumental Brasses* by Herbert Haines, the earlier date of about 1370 is given. Perhaps it is the lack of 'remarkableness' of this plain representation of a bearded man of his day, with the hood for warmth or shelter (still preserved for us in academic garb), the long, close-fitting sleeves garnished with many buttons, even the characteristic hair-cut—that makes it not too difficult to imagine him and his fellows, worshippers here in the parish church.

....

The medieval church was probably at its most gorgeous and the enthusiasm of its congregation at its height when various bequests were made by wills between 1523 and 1543 for the maintenance of the altars and chantries and their lights. Those enumerated were "All Hallows Chapel", "Our'Lady's Altar", "St. Catherine's Altar" and "St. Margaret's Altar". There is mention too of bequests to St. Thomas's light, the four principal lights and the Rood light. The Rev. E. Marshall who collected these particulars also quotes from the will of William Pope, proved May 11th, 1523, (father of Sir Thomas, the celebrated founder of Trinity College, Oxford) :—"Item, I bequeathe to the torchis, the belles, our Ladie beame, St. Thomas beame, to everyche one of them iijs iiiijd," (3s. and 4d.).

We can only now locate two of these Altars, that to the Blessed Virgin would, of course be in the north aisle where there remains a shelf and a niche, the last apparently to hold her statue.

The south aisle is still dedicated to St. Thomas—St. Thomas à Becket doubtless, the people's hero. Both aisles at the east ends have each on their south side the piscinas used for washing the sacred vessels of the Mass.

Contemporary with these bequests is the altar tomb in the Lady Chapel sacred to the memory of William Bylling, wool merchant of the Staple of Calais, and his wife Elizabeth. The original brass inlay of a crucifix and two kneeling figures has been mutilated but the brass inscription beneath is only partially broken, and reads in 'Old English' lettering :—

"Of youre charity praye for the soule of Willm Bylling, m'chnt of the Staple, at Calays, which decessyd the 28th daye of Auguste, ano 1533. And for the soule of Elizabeth, hys wyfe, which decessyd the ......daye of......ber ano 1522."

Close on a century prior to this, the Fraternity or Guild of the Holy Trinity was instituted. As it was a very representative body, holding land in Deddington and Clifton, and having an important place in the Church with additional clergy for its services, the full particulars from Marshall's notes are of interest.

'In 1445, according to the enrolment in the Record Office, letters patent were granted on the petition of John Somerton, John Collis, William Horncastell, William Tommes, Clement Draper, John Collyns and Richard Maynard, of Deddington, by which it was granted to them to found or establish a guild, as aforesaid, for that is the name (of the Holy Trinity) which it is commonly found to have. The Guild was to consist of a Warden, or Master, to be elected annually by the members on the Vigil or Feast of the Holy Trinity, and the brethren or sisters, being of Deddington, together with any others admitted by them ; it was to be a corporation with a common seal and perpetual succession. The Warden and his successors were to sue or be sued, in the name of the Warden or Master of the Fraternity or Guild of the Holy Trinity of Deddington ; and further, the Guild was empowered after its institution to found a chantry for two chaplains to celebrate at the altars of the Holy Trinity and of the Blessed Virgin in the church, as well for the healthful state of the members of the Guild while living, and of their souls when they shall have deceased, as for King Henry VI and Queen Margaret, and their predecessors and successors, in like manner ; according to the usual form of such letters patent......The chantry was to have the right to hold lands and other property of the yearly value of £12, the statute of Mortmain notwithstanding.'

For the first Warden, John Andrew, and his wife Lucy, the chaplains were specially to pray. John Sparks, by his Will, dated 1543, and William Payne, by his Will, dated 1544, both bequeathed 3s. and 4d. respectively, 'to be brothers of the Guild, and their souls to be prayed for.'

On the dissolution of the chantries, this one became part of the Duchy of Lancaster. The old Deed whereby the Guild was dissolved, dated December 1635, is in the possession of Mr. Henry E. Stilgoe, and by his courtesy a copy transcribed from it is in the appendix.

Among the many beauties and features of interest in the church, which remain practically uninjured and unaltered by the catastrophic fall of tower and bells, are the north porch of 15th century work with dome-shaped roof and 'fan' tracery; the piscina and sedilia (seats for three clergy) in the chancel, and a strikingly beautiful perpendicular window cut in the south wall, almost above the stone effigy in St. Thomas's chapel. Behind this altar there are some unglazed red tiles of an early date, hidden by the drapery and framework.

THE FALL OF THE TOWER, AND THE BEGINNING OF THE REGISTERS.

The first entry in volume one of the Deddington registers is March 25th, 1631, it having been transcribed with others from registers presumably destroyed or damaged in the fall of the church tower. It opens with flourishes of the pen and the dramatic sentence :—

"This book was bought the yere whch the tower fell 1634."

The names of the churchwardens heading it are Wm. Brudnell and James Apletree. In 1654 Edward Kempster, registrar (1654), Parish clerk (1658), Schoolmaster (1672) makes his appearance therein. He died in 1676, leaving behind him the reputation of an honest, painstaking official, and many valuable notes on the events of his time. His appointment as registrar is thus given near the end of book I.

"Thomas Apletree.

"Whereas it appears unto me by a certificate dated the 14th of August, instant (1653) made by the hand of the Maior [Bailiff ?] and of the Inhabitants of Daddington (and the parish) in the county of Oxon whoe are chargeable towards the releife of the Poore of the said Parish that Edward Kempster of Daddington aforesd. is by them the said Inhabitants Chosen register of the Parish aforesd., I therefore (by virtue of the late Act of Parliament made touching Marriages and Registring thereof dated the 24th August 1653) have sworne the said Edward Kempster to execute the said Registers office for the Towne and Parish of daddington aforesd. as by the Act is directed and required, And doe also Authorise the said Edward Kempster to receive such ffees in the execution of his said office, as by the said act is Allowed.

Given under my hand and Seale the fifteenth day of August 1654.

Signed   Tho Apletree."

(It is curious to note that every entry of the Apletree or Kempster families is encircled with red ink !)

Kempster's next preferment is briefly stated "Edward Kempster began to be clerk this fifth September 1658."

The Commonwealth extended from 1649 to 1660, and Kempster's strong Royalist sympathies which are evidenced by a note in his hand, presently to be quoted, must have been severely affronted by historical and other events, notably the innovation of 'crying banns' in the very market place of his town.

Here is his note on the Restoration :—"His Majestie Charles ye second Came into London ye 29th of May 1660 wch was ye 12th yeare of his reign wch was Brought in wthout Blood shedd and his ffather was put to Death ye 30th of January 1648—by the tyrannicall powers of Oliver Cromwell who dyed September ye 3, 1658 and was taken up after he had bin buried 2 yeare and above and was hanged at tiborne and his head was sett up at Westminster and his body was buried underneath Tyburne 1661 wch Oliver did governe heare some years in England."

The events that must have been upsetting to a conservative and orthodox Registrar were the marriages, of which the validity was authorised under the very act of 1653 quoted in Kempster's appointment. One is recorded in the Parish registers of Woodstock. "1657. Alexander Hautinge, husbandman, and Marie Prentice, Sprinstresse, both of the Parish of Badington (sic), in the county of Oxon., were married upon the 29 of December, by Mr. Thomas Rayer, Justice of the Peace for this in-corporation."

It is entered in the Deddington register as follows :—"Alexander Hawtin and Mary Prentice were married ye 29 day of December 1657, by Thomas Rayer, Justice of ye Peace for ye burrow of New Woodstock, and by Mr. Jones, minister of Woodstock aforesd., and weare published by me three markett dayes in ye markett place in Dadington, yt is to say on ye 12th and on ye 19th and on ye 26th days, being all in December aforesd."

The practice of a civil ceremony and its subsequent solemnization by a minister is one, of course, customary in some continental countries, and perfectly valid here now.

Edward Kempster's historical sense, to which we are indebted, is further instanced by a note he makes on the occasion of a burial : "Hannah Wyer, daughter of Mr. James Wyer, wch was minister of this towne when Charles ye Scd came home in to England, was buried June ye 13th, 1670."

Kempster, himself, died during the vicariate of Jeremiah Wheate, whose 'amiable spouse', as recorded on her gravestone in the chancel, bore him fifteen sons and six daughters. She died in 1685 at the incredibly (considering the circumstances !) early age of thirty-two. Hannah Wheate is buried with one of her twins.

Another of the seven vicars, or ministers, under whom Edward Kempster served was James Wyer, 1660-1664. Ten years later there is this entry in the register :—"Hannah Wyer, daughter of Mr. James Wyer......" etc., as quoted above.

Kempster was Registrar, Parish clerk and Schoolmaster—"on February 15th, 1672, the school-house was made in the church for Edward Kempster to teach there," (entry in register of that date). He had a hand in most parish affairs, but the absorbing concerns for him must always have been the fortunes of the Stuarts, the restoration of the church tower, and the reparation of the damage done to the building and the bells in its fall.

Mr. Marshall refers to the disaster in these words :—'In March, 1635, that is 1634 O.S. (i.e. Old Style, before the reformation of the calendar), the tower of the church fell, and injured at the same time a portion of the fabric. The injury done amounted to the estimated sum of £8,250, and letters patent were granted in the following year, which authorized a collection in all churches and chapels for raising this amount "for repairing the tower and parish church of Deddington." Some years later a question arose upon the expenditure and a petition was presented to the council by (? Edward) Kempster of Deddington ; when it was ordered that it should be referred to the Bishop of Oxford to call the petitioner and the collector before him, and examine whether the letters patent warrant the giving any part of the money for the relief of the petitioner......The repairs, however, remained for a long time incomplete, and in consequence of this, on January 21st, 1643, the king sent an order from Oxford, to the parson, churchwardens, and others, in these terms :—

"Whereas information is given to us that by the fall of your steeple......the bells are made unserviceable for you, till the same be rebuilt and they are new founded ; ......we hereby require you to send the same to our magazine here in New College......the just weight and nature of them be ascertained......to the end we may restore the same in materials or monies to your church, when you shall have occasion to use the same." And so they became munitions of war.

According to the insription on the smallest bell which reads "Antony Basely. Richard Large. C.W.1649", Deddington did not wait long for the ting-tang, which can only be chimed, not rung, as it is on a half-wheel. The six large bells constituting the peal seem to have been all cast at the same time ; the inscription on them is : "Thos. Mears, late Lester, Pack and Chapman of London, fecit, 1791." The foundry was at Whitechapel. The firm of Mears still casts bells. The curfew is sounded on the fourth bell.

The collection authorised in other churches for the restoration of our St. Peter's and St. Paul's, follows a custom prevalent in the 17th century, and till the middle of the 19th. In the Oxford Diocesan Magazine for November 1928, the Rev. Maurice Frost, Vicar of Deddington, has collected a number of 'briefs'—letters patent authorising a collection—among which is one 'colected at Dadington for Tosceter 0-10-0 (Sept. ye 15, 1672).' Other instances of Deddington's generosity occur in the Registers. As, for instance, these two, in which also history is mirrored :—"Collected for the Poore visited by pestilence (the plague) March, 1665. 10/8 - 3/11."

"October ye 10th 1666. Collected for the sad fire, which happened the 2nd day of September at London. £1.16.8."

Another is very eloquent. "1670. November 21st. Collected towards the redeeming of our English from slavery (? the galleys) £4.1.7."

On March 26th 1671, is the entry of a sum collected for 'two Hungarians', which is puzzling, though again generous.

The present font is new (1841) but the registers commemorate the previous one in this wise :—"John West the sonne of Samuel and Sarah was baptized March the 6th being the first that was baptized in the Vante 1663."

The keeping of registers by all parishes was made compulsory in 1538, and in 1597 it was decreed that they must be copied on parchment. Our early registers are of vellum bound in soft undressed leather. The ink is surprisingly little faded and the script —particularly Kempster's—clear. Naturally they deal with all manner of people, but invariably entries of burials between the years 1667 and 1814 are followed by the declaration on oath that such and such a person 'according to Act of Parliament on affidavit' was buried in woollen—this being a law for the encouragement of the industry.

Misery and poverty are reflected in this entry : "Richard a base childe sonne of   (left blank)   Ason borne within ye parish of Barford St Johns ye woman being delivered on ye other side of ye brooke whin ye field of the said Barford St Johns neere unto a mill commonly knowne and called by the name of Barford Mill and being brought into the said mill did here abide untill ye said chylde was baptized within this pish (parish) and that by direction of the ordinary ye XXVIth day of July anno dmi 1640."

The burial of John Cary, gentleman, member of a well-known local family, several of whose gravestones help to pave the vestry, brings a certain melancholy of fashion into the register for he was killed in a duel in Hyde Park. The entry reads :—

"John Cary, gentleman, 1695 : burial : ye son of Mr. ffrancis Henry Cary, was buried July ye 4th and John Cawson of Great St. Bartholomews London made oath yt he was buried in Wollen according to ye Act of Parliament, which said John was basely killed in a duel in Hyd. Park June ye 23rd. His Mother was ye daughter of Tho. Apletree Esq. of this town."

....

The great change in the attitude of church-goers, from the medieval to the Georgian and early Victorian eras, was a literal one. Members of the first period sought to view the altars. From Queen Anne's day and for many generations, they wished to face the pulpit, which developed into a three-decker, and hear well. On that account there was considerable competition for seats in the east end of the north aisle, which then altarless, was a sort of cosy corner much in request. Mr. H. E. Stilgoe contributes some interesting instances of 'Faculties' which testify to this :—

"A faculty was granted 17th December 1728, to John Appletree of Deddington, Apothecary, for appropriating the seat in the north east corner of the north isle of the said parish church adjoining on the south to the seat there in the possession of Job Coles and on the west to a seat in the possession of several of the parish, which seat stands upon the burying place of the family of the Belchers, to the sole use of the said John Appletree and his family during their continuance in the said parish, who upon his leaving the said parish gave up the said seat to the said Nathaniel Stilgoe to which he and his family have ever since resorted without interruption, etc."

"A faculty was granted the 24th December 1784 in respect of this same pew to Susannah Bissell, Widow, the occupier of a mansion house, belonging to Nathaniel Stilgoe on the east side of New Street." It adjoins Ilbury House and is now occupied by Mr. Wood Page.

"It is interesting to note," remarks Mr. Stilgoe, "that John Appletree, Apothecary, had his seat over the burying place of Samuel Belcher, Apothecary."

These were, of course, the old 'horse-box' pews which Joseph Wilkin's drawings, hung under the tower, depict. In them the parish notables dozed when inclined, though the parish beadle rapped soundly the lesser sort caught napping.

Mr. Stilgoe has noted that the living apthecary's seat was above the deceased apothecary's final resting place. This was the Samuel Belcher who, in 1668, issued his trading token adorned with the Apothecaries' Arms. A mural tablet in the north aisle records his death on December 9th, 1688 and his motto : "Loyall au Mort." An inscription to the memory of Elizabeth the wife of Thomas Belcher (the name is sometimes spelt Belchier) is dated December 22nd, 1718. William, son of Samuel Belchier, was also buried here in 1682, their family vault, initialled 'S.B.', taking up considerable space in the flooring.

In fact it might be called a chapel almost sacred to the medical faculty, for the beautiful stained glass window by H. J. Davies, executed by the Bromsgrove Guild, Worcestershire, depicting the Assumption of the Blessed Virgin, with on the lower panels the Annunciation and the figures of Hannah, mother of Samuel, and of St. George either side, unveiled in June 1924, was to the memory of the first wife of Dr. George Horatio Jones and of her mother and brother.

This chapel contains the graves of the Nutt family (Job Nutt issued a trading token). On the wall is a marble tablet erected by the 'afflicted parents' of George Brodrick, of Macclesfield, who at the age of 19, when journeying to take up his residence at Brasenose College, 'was killed by the overturning of the coach at the entrance to the town of Deddington'—crossroads which were a danger spot then as now.

Before passing on to the restored church in its latest phase it will be well to remember once more the importance it had conferred on it by being made head of a deanery. Mr. Manchip in his 'Notes on Deddington' draws attention to the fact that the "Decanatus de Dadynton" occurs in the Taxation of Pope Nicholas IV, A.D.1291, one of the earlier publications of the Commissioners of Public Records. Deddington, as head of a deanery which includes 28 parishes, Banbury being one, possessed a real claim to be helped to build itself up and refurnish the belfry. By virtue of decanal authority courts to try offenders were held, described in the previous chapter, within the church precincts. Probably it last figured in relation to justice in the case related in the Windsor Court Rolls, given as follows :—

"Appointment by the Dean and Canons (of Windsor) of William Wilson, Charles Sonnibank, Edmund Nuthall, doctors in divinity, their attorneys to demand the payment on the last day of the six weeks of the wheat according to lease 18 August 1567. Endorsed. A demand was made by Dr. Sonnebank and Dr. Nuthall at the south doore on Thursday being 6th May 1613 about half an hour before sunsetting, and continued demanding the said wheat till the sun was set, but no wheat was tendered."

....

They built the new tower very stout and strong. Some find fault with its high, sturdy buttresses as tending to clumsiness. But parishioners with experience of raising money towards expensive repairs will sympathise and say, "No wonder !" The stone figures of the patron saints on the tower are of the date of the rebuilding.

Much of the restoration work inside is good, the tall arch at the west end leading from, or under, the tower particularly so : but later, taste deteriorated culminating about the middle of the 19th century, when the editor of the Gazateer for Oxfordshire, year 1852, is led to protest in a manner rare in his epoch. After remarking on the 'striking interior' and 'beautiful arches', he says, 'the view is however disfigured by an unsightly gallery of unpainted deal in the west corner of the south aisle, erected to supply a temporary necessity caused by the residence of a popular preacher (the Rev. R. Greaves, also his curate Hughes, see Part II of Chapter "Deddington Folk")......The walls are covered by thick coats of whitewash and until lately the beautiful tracery...was hid beneath an accumulation of rubbish......" A contempory also reported ivy as thrusting itself through interstices in the wall of the south aisle. But rescue from most of these ills was soon to come through the Rev. William Cotton Risley, Vicar from 1836 to 1848, when he resigned. The Rev. Thomas Boniface (1878, resigned 1924) also made the good state of the church his care, and the present organ, built by Binns of Leeds, and considered a remarkably fine instrument for its size, remains a monument to the taste and enthusiasm of Mr. Boniface and his congregation who raised upwards of £600 for the purpose. It was dedicated by Bishop Richardson (formerly Bishop of Zanzibar) on August 20th, 1912. The Rev. Maurice Frost, now Vicar, has been responsible for big efforts to renew a great part of the roof, and to re-hang the bells—the last being accomplished in 1929. The church's last achievement, under him, has been the substitution of blue Hornton stone in the sanctuary for extremely ugly tiling, and removal of the latter from an interesting series of gravestone, also in the chancel, many of them inscribed with names of the important family of Apletree.

The ivy which was described as invading the south aisle was evidently part of that which, mantling the tower, became a danger to the integrity of its mortar. Mr. Duffell Faulkner, whose interest in antiquities very properly extended to the church, is reported to have said that any renovations or improvements would have no support from him till the ivy was taken down. Accordingly this was done, and since then the tower has stood safe and bare.

The vicarage house opposite the south porch is a plain stone building about 100 years old. The Castle House, which sometimes goes by the name of the 'Old Parsonage' is generally agreed to be the resting place of Charles I, referred to as 'The Parsonage House' where he lay for one night during a royal progress through Oxon and Bucks in 1644. That there was a vicarage prior to the present one, and subsequent to the 'Old Parsonage' of royal fame, is amply proved by these extracts from the Windsor Manor Court Rolls :—
"They will pay the Vicar £36.6.8 and spend £141.9.4. on the Vicarage house and they will hold the ground on which the old Vicarage stood and pay the Vicar therefor £3.13.4. 18 March 1680."

And in the same Rolls, this is signed by Francis Henry Cary and William Draper on Dec. 17, 1701 :—"To the Vicar £36.6.8. (£141.9.4 was laid out for rebuilding Vicarage) that land now held by present lessees at will of Vicar for £3.13.4......" Virtually a repetition of the first statement, except that it is plain that after an interval of 21 years the deed of rebuilding had been done."

A statement in the list of Quit Rents, dated June 14, 1710 (payable yearly), gives among the leaseholders, Z. Stilgoe as paying £10.0.0 for 'The Parsonage House and Vicarage garden', which may be taken as proof that the Parsonage House was the Great House of the Award Map, and the Vicarage quite a separate dwelling, with more extensive grounds than required which the Vicar leased at the rental of £3.13.4.

3. STREETS AND HOUSES.

The heart of Deddington is its Market Place, and presiding over this—with due respect to the over-lordship of the Parish Church nearby—is the Town Hall. It is a quaint small structure rather continental in appearance, particularly in its setting of bleak, empty space. "How French looking!" one feels inclined to exclaim. It has stood there for at least three centuries, though the red and white-ness of the exterior is evidently newish. Formerly there were shops below, the rents going to pay for the tax called 'fifteenths' which was for the relief of the poor.

Mr. William Wing, whose 'Supplement to Marshall's Deddington' reprinted from the 'Oxford Chronicle' in 1879, is a rare and interesting pamphlet, relates :—'for many years the Petty Sessions of the district were held in the diminutive room of the King's Arms Inn, a space of most inadequate dimensions. Afterwards these meetings were transferred to the upper room of the Town Hall, but this arrangement was unsatisfactory, as it was necessary to eject the public whenever the magistrates had to debate any point in private. This inconvenience is now obviated, as the magistrates have a retiring room at the Police Station erected at the expense of the County......The Town Hall still serves many useful public purposes, and its upper room is used as a reading chamber, well supplied with books and newspapers. The lower portion has thrice been converted into a polling hustings at contested county elections in 1837, 1852 and 1862.'

The fire-engine is now housed below, having been removed from a building on the Green at present the storage place of street lamp glasses, which, divorced from their sadly rusting posts, mark an era hopeful of more gaslight. The engine is convenient for the Town well whose spring once supplied the Town pool that was so notable a feature before it was filled in more than half a century ago.

Mr. Edward Mullis the saddler of those days (his granddaughter still lives in the same house) was famous for pulling children out of the Pool which his workshop overlooked. There were railings round and the children swung on them, frequently toppling into the water. The formation of the ground near the well is a fair indication of the hollow of the Pool, though on the near side to the houses it was further from the path than might appear, a cart and horse having room to drive round with ease.

Looking about one in Market Square it is evident that 'the land of gold' impression made on the writer (Mr. Frederick L. Griggs) of 'Highways and Byways in Oxford and the Cotswolds' by

Deddington's 'rich golden' brown stone has succumbed greatly to red brick, blue slate, and what Mr. Griggs calls sarcastically 'the simple early Gothic of yesterday'. The Town Hall, itself, excuses by its quaintness an altered complexion ; but what can be said of the big block, once a warehouse, behind it, except that any speedy form of disappearance—without injury to the inhabitants—is ardently to be desired ?

The taste which condemned our thatched houses as contributing to the 'somewhat mean appearance' of the town 'largely built of that brown stone plentifully found in the immediate neighbourhood' (Oxfordshire Gazette of 1852) has left many marks, the beautiful Stonesfield roofing as well as the despised thatch being continually replaced by slate, pink asbestos, or worse, by corrugated zinc. Yet in spite of all there is enough left of the unspoiled to rejoice eye and heart with beauty.

A curious example of the transition of this original harmony into the 'simple early Gothic of yesterday' which Mr. Griggs deprecates, is the strange case of 'Pretoria' at the curving of Hudson Street into Market Square. It bears its history in its name. Deddington celebrated the Relief of Mafeking by burning President Kreuger in effigy on a big bonfire. The wind got up and in spite of every effort sparks were carried to the thatched roof of the farmhouse on 'Pretoria's' site and on to the gate into the yard, which formerly had a lovely thatched shelter above it like the old one still existing in Philcote Street. 'Oom Paul' on the bonfire took a neat revenge in the building's complete destruction and its blight rests upon a house reconstructed of the old materials—yes—but with the difference conferred by 1905.

Crossing the Square again and standing back to that palish red block with its warehouse history one faces a grass plot with a fair open space beyond. That is the Bull Ring where baiting took place. For a description of this form of 'sport' one cannot do better than read Mary Webb's in her Shropshire novel 'Precious Bane.' One knows not whether to pity most, the bull, the dogs or the onlookers who enjoyed it.

THE CASTLE HOUSE.

From this spot there is a good view of the Castle House, Old Parsonage, Rectorial Farm, or Great House—for all are names ascribed to that stately Jacobean Manor-house-like dwelling, and each embalms something of its story. Skelton's 'Antiquities of Oxford' (1823) calls it the Rectorial Farm House, and a charming vignette on page 17 of that work depicts the north side of the church and shows the farm out-buildings, excrescences on the original, which is of entirely different style and period. The Rev. E. Marshall, whose 'Notes' on our locality are at once the fullest and most learned, identifies Castle House with the Great House, so-called in the Inclosure Award. Its situation close to the church—a wall only separates it from the churchyard—traces of foundations that show that there was a larger ancient house before the present ; its capacious tithes barn in the grounds, and the private chapel or oratory dating from pre-reformation times within, all give it an almost overwhelming claim to be the 'Old Parsonage' too. Mr. Marshall on page 12 of the 'Notes' states that this 'ancient rectorial house of the sixteenth century' is on the estate given to the Deans and Canons of Windsor when the Windsor Manor was formed by royal license at request of William de Bohun, patron of the church, in 1351—a grant having a permanent effect on the condition of Deddington. In 1879 the occupier was Mr. Thomas Gardner. Another farmer succeeded him named Simpson, who married a member of the well-known Appletree family, and it is significant that an 'A' is on the leaden pipe-heads. The main gate formerly opened on to Victoria Terrace and stables and coach-house were on that side.

It is the romance of history which this old house enshrines for us. Charles I is stated by Sir Edward Walker in attendance on the king, to have 'slept at the Parsonage' when he 'lay at Dedington'. The occasion was after the battle of Cropredy which took place on June 29th, 1644, with success to the Royalists. That day was a Saturday and on the Monday following Charles proceeded to Aynho and then crossed the Cherwell. Mr. Marshall quotes from the Diary of Captain Symonds, an officer in the king's service the following :—

"Munday morning, about four of the clock, his majestie, with all his army, drum beating, colours flying, and trumpets sounding, marched through Middleton Cheney, from thence to Farmigo, where Sir Roland Egerton hath a howse ; from thence by Aynoe-on-the-hill to where Lord Wilmott hath a faire seat. Here a trumpett of Waller came, and exchanged 60 and od prisoners of ours taken, which were all they took, wee having a hundred more. The king lay at Dedington. From Dedington the army marched Tuesday morning, by where the Lord Viscount Falkland hath a faire howse......"

The Rev. E. Marshall continues—'Deddington was often occupied by troops, as one of the outposts of the contending armies, during the course of the civil war, so that it must have had a frequent share in the events of that troublous time.'

The Oxfordshire Gazateer (1852) while dignifying Castle House as 'an architectural curiosity' dismisses it with these few words :—

'Near the church is an old house, consisting of a square tower with open stone balustrade at top, which is now the residence of a furmor, and the property of the dean and canons of Windsor. An upper apartment in this tower is said to have been used as an oratory in Catholic times.' It does not connect it with the visit of King Charles though citing his majesty as having slept at a Parsonage house which certainly could not have been our Vicarage facing the Church's west front, which is little more than 100 years old.

The oratory, or Chapel, seems to date from the 'Decorated' period like other relics of Deddington's days of ecclesiastical fame— a history mostly told in stones, for its written lore has great gaps. This chapel has every equipment for due celebration of the Mass. Underneath is a priest's hole or hiding place, a reminder of the religious intolerance which so cruelly penalised holders of the old faith. This part of the country possesses many such witnesses to the existence of old Catholic families. It may, like others more renowned, have been constructed by the Jesuit Nicholas Owen, called "little John", who died on the rack rather than reveal the secret of those refuges.

Many have been the vicissitudes of this admired house. The list of quit rents for 1710 show Zachariah Stilgoe paying £10 as leaseholder of the 'Parsonage house and garden and Vicaridge garden' (probably where an older vicarage had stood). Mr. Thomas Smith remembers as a boy that a winnowing machine was in one noble panelled room, while another was used as a granary ! Mr. Robert Franklin of the famous church restoration firm, actually rescued it from its debased condition. In 1894 he put back the balustrade which had been taken down, and he bought the property from the Ecclesiastical Commissioners. With the assistance of Garner, the noted architect, then living at Fritwell Manor, it was made once again the dignified dwelling typical of pure domestic taste. The "Banbury Guardian" in an article at the time of Franklin's restoration, states that "it was in this house that Sir Thomas Pope, founder of Trinity College, is believed to have been born."

In the Autumn of 1925 it suffered severely from fire, supposed to have been caused by the decaying of cement several hundred years' old which thus exposed a chimney beam to the heat. Thanks to the efforts of Mr. Herbert Long, the present owner, such portions as were damaged have been perfectly restored, not only in the materials but in the spirit of their past.

Three ways directly lead out of the Market Place into the Oxford-Banbury high-road. One is along the Horse Fair, the other by Hudson's Street or Lane, and the third midway between those passing beneath archways at either end is the Tchure. There is nothing remarkable about this last narrow thoroughfare except its name, which is doubtful in origin but has a counterpart in Banbury, so possibly is peculiar to this part of the county. One explanation offered is that it signifies a bond or passage between streets, though no root-term is apparent to the non-expert.

The Rev. Obed Parker, Congregational minister, had his chapel here ; it is now the Foresters' Hall and can be hired for meetings and lectures.

Before leaving the Market Square note should be taken of the 'Hermitage', a house mainly Queen Anne but with obvious signs of its earlier Jacobean foundation in the dormer windows ; one blocked-out gazes blindly from the wall which evidently marked where it originally ended leaving space for the 'Quadrangle' that used to exist between the Red Lion across to the King's Arms. In its garden extension the other side of the Horse Fair was the true hermitage from which the house is called.

Mr. Duffel Faulkner, Deddington's antiquarian lawyer who lived in Hudson's Lane, is quoted by the Rev. E. Marshall as writing some sixty years ago :—

"A building of this name (Hermitage) still exists in the garden near the school..." Mr. Marshall goes on to say that "such a place of prayer was not an uncommon appendage to a town," informing us further that Beesley's History of Banbury quotes the Will of Nicholas Woodhull (1531) which directs that the 'Hermitage at the Briggfoot of Banbury' should be repaired and 'an honest man' put in it to pray for himself and his friends.

The hermitage, situated where indicated, would be contiguous to the famous Pilgrim's Rest House, adding to that 'religious atmosphere' which our many shrines and chantries ought surely to have promoted.

High Street, beginning at the Horse Fair corner and changing into New Street where Hudson's Lane crosses it, varies farm-houses with a few shops and private dwellings. Taking this whole stretch it is astonishing what a number of farms once bordered it, for even those in private occupation are mostly just farm-houses transformed. There was a somewhat similar evolution in the case of the 'solid handsome stone mansion' much admired by the 'Gazeteer' of 1852, which the Rev. W. Cotton Risley refaced, heightened and added to, only leaving one wing and a small portion of back elevation still showing the old Cotswold Stone.

Across the way, next the 'Old Bakery' of pudding pie fame, is a pretty, homely stone house which a faculty (Dec. 4th, 1784) for granting its occupant Mrs. Susannah Bissell, use of a pew, pompously calls 'a mansion house' too. Adjoining that a much larger edifice with Queen Anne or early Georgian face upon a Jacobean structure, is the property of Dr. G. H. Jones. Originally belonging to Christ Church College it exhibits the characteristic of that establishment's fondness for white plaster renovations, which, however, time and creepers have here almost obliterated. Hence, though, its name more than fifty years back, of the 'White House'. Since then Mr. Slatter, who had retired from Ilbury Farm, re-christened it 'Ilbury House.'

Formerly Mr. Henry Churchill, coroner, resided there, the room above the arch still showing traces of an orifice in the ceiling through which clerks over-head in the top storey used to shoot papers for examination or signature into the lawyer's office below. Between the Churchill and Slatter occupancy a ladies' school was kept here by the Misses Miller, and the Misses Caroline and Mary Ann Bryant respectively. Since then it has seen manifold changes —the taking down of attics above the kitchen wing, and the absorption of Franklin's old timber-yard into its grounds. In a line with Ilbury House is a comely couple of small houses in the native brown stone. The first of these was once a Post Office, and extending to the rear were a set of buildings where post-master and printer J. Calcutt turned out bill-heads, etc. His name is in the directories for 1852.

An aperture plainly felt in the wall of the front sitting-room still marks where the post-box was. And on another of its walls, stripped some years ago for re-papering, boldly scrawled across the plaster was the following record of a regrettable page in the town's past—

'This day the bell ropes of Deddington Church pawned for drink.'

This indignant outburst was from the pencil of a tenant who was a non-conformist apparently of considerable means, for he was minded to buy land adjoining Deddington House on the north for the site of a chapel. But the Rev. Cotton Risley out-bid him and made it a kitchen garden. A congregational chapel was subsquent-ly erected in the same street further away. Behind these lies the 'Park' often referred to in transfers of property. It is cut up into fields and paddocks but its beautiful undulations are park-like indeed.

LEADEN PORCH.

Leaden Porch House, in ancient documents simply 'Leaden Porch', is the most interesting building in New Street. Several mentions of it are made in the Court Rolls of Deddington in possession of the Dean and Canons of St. George's Free Chapel, Windsor, also called 'Rolls of Court Baron of the Dean and Canons', etc. The Courts Baron were held in Deddington. One extract states that John Stampe of West Eldesley in the County of Berks, gent., acquired leases of the following properties :—'the rectory, manor, castle (i.e. the site of the castle) and the park and the capital messuage or tenement called Ledon Porch.' Signed and dated 10th Feb., 1570.

Another Deed dated 20th June, 1666, grants to 'Thomas Appletree of Deddington (Dadyngton), Esquire, and Thomas Appletree, his son and heir apparent for 20s. lease for one year at peppercorn rents to Dean and Canons......the Leaden Porch, in a certain street leading into Oxford the East field and the West field, called the Windsor, and all on the West side of Stonebridge, called the Fisheries, the Castle closes, 10 acres and all the Manor, signed by both.'

A surrender of Lease by Henry Cary, rector of Brinkworth, Wilts and William Draper of Nether Worton to Sir James Chamberlaine, Bart. and Edward Lovedon, details the properties rents and conditions as follows :—'The Rectory, Manor, Castle and park, Leaden Porch for £56.6.8. (i.e. for the rectory £32, for the Manor, Castle and park, Leaden Porch for £24.6.8) and 3 quarters and 6 bushels of wheat to be judged by the Steward, Treasurer or Charter for which the Dean and Canons will pay £14.14.0. keep Court rolls, providing lodging for three nights and two days and when they don't come 40s.'

Signed by Cary and Draper Dec. 17th, 1701.

In 1714, as leaseholder of Leaden Porch Farm House, George French pays £9, and for two yard lands part of the same farm £24.10.0.

The earliest mention of all is the most interesting as recording the passing of the lease of 'lands in Dadyngton, lately purchased of the said John Bustard (of Adderbury) of Thomas Pope, and also his moiety of the Parsonage, tythe and demesne land of the Parsonage and also of the domination or lordship of the Dean and Chapter's called Leaden Porch for 21 years, rent £11' etc., to John Edmunds, 20th December, 1534.

Thus Leaden Porch House is undoubtedly linked with the founder of Trinity College, Oxford, Deddington's greatest man

Anyone passing by it will note that it is beautiful, of the richest coloured Cotswold stone, but of a leaden porch there is now no vestige. But, most arresting, the arched doorway with 'bosses' is massive and grooved, resembling somewhat the archway of the Exhibition inn—perhaps part of an older Leaden Porch House ; perhaps even spoils from the demolition of the Castle may have contributed this and the remarkable window to one side of the door, evidently inserted, to which experts have assigned a date as early as John's reign.

Further in the Oxford direction a monotonous row of cottages marks the time when every parish had to support its own paupers before the passing of the Poor Law Act. The pauper inmates were lodged in the first part of this row, the cottages communicating, and the Master and Mistress were housed in the rather more commodious dwelling at the further (Oxford direction) end. Wing states in his supplement :—

"When the Poor Law Unions were formed it was at first hoped that Deddington would be a centre, but as a sufficiency of parishes could not be found without going into Northamptonshire, and Mr. Cartwright was strongly opposed to such a step, the idea was abandoned, and Deddington was tacked on to Woodstock, to which applicants for relief have to take a walk ten miles each way, if required to appear before the Guardians assembled in the Boardroom, and if this is not *cruelty* I cannot define the word.

'Deddington and its two hamlets were at first treated as three separate poor-law parishes, the former returning two guardians, the two others one each ; but as a trial at Nisi Prius shortly afterwards revealed that the parish is all one, four guardians are now chosen yearly for the whole area. An attempt to dismember parts of the Woodstock and Bicester Unions, and so to constitute a Deddington Union in 1858, was supported by the parishes of Deddington and Over Worton, but opposed so strongly by all the other places interested, that the project fell through ; the ratepayers who had paid for the erection of one workhouse were unwilling to pay for another.'

'Before the passing of the Union Chargeability Act (says Mr. Wing in another part of his pamphlet) injuries were inflicted on Deddington and its hamlets by the owners of neighbouring parishes ejecting their poor and enforcing them into Deddington poor-rates, etc.' A moment's reflection will bring home that the injuries were not to ratepayers alone, but to the unfortunate beings thus pushed out into unwilling hands.

Today the 'cruelty of compelling applicants for poor relief to walk to Woodstock' is somewhat mitigated, the centre having been transferred to Banbury, four miles nearer.

Opposite to this one-time poor-house row is a stable of chapel-like design. Once a little Bethel, later Salvation Army barracks, this building has still preserved the gateway leading to the former vestry and the door by which its small congregation went in, though the steps to it have gone and the flooring has been lifted to serve as a hayloft.

Satin, Saturn or Satan Lane (it is 'Sotty Lane' in the Latin Rolls of 1424 when the Prior of Bicester granted a 'toft' in the Reekyard, or rickyard hard by it, to Walter Cheyne, Vicar), branches towards the town again after a fine high spur of golden wall that marks the approach from Oxford. It is now St. Thomas' Street.

In Satin Lane behind Hopcraft's Yard was once the village school, and at foot of the pleasant green, known as Goose's Green, was a rope-walk. Franklin's timber yard opened into Philcote Street, which in the 1710 list of quit rents figures as 'Pilsock' Street.

In Church Lane, built about 1818 by the feoffees of the Charities of the Parish, is a quaint neat row of Almshouses which accommodate four poor men and four poor women, who receive (the men) four shillings weekly, and the women three shillings.

Wing remarks in his Supplement that 'the state of the footpaths is far from satisfactory.' They are now in excellent order, with a few specimens left—notably the rocky rough blocks against the churchyard wall by main entrance—to prove the truthfulness of Mr. Wing. The majority of the old stones removed are now living well up to their name as 'crazy' paving in the grounds of Dr. Jones. In that same garden too are old stone steps and a small trough rescued from the ruins of the Pest House on the Banbury road where in a hollow of a field to the left (going north) a cattle shed now stanes. In the stone trough, it is said, coins from the Pest House used to be placed. being passed through water in a primitive attempt at disinfection.

Passing along Council Street towards Castle Green a low stone house of considerable charm, with a very long shaped diamond-paned window under the eaves on the near side, attracts attention. It bears dates 1655, 1735 and 1917, the last two with initials Z.S. (Zachariah Stilgoe) and H.E.S. respectively.

Mr. H. E. Stilgoe supplies some interesting information connected with it. Quoting from the Will of Anthony Stilgoe, 1606, he writes that the testator bequeathed to Elizabeth his wife "a house situate in 'Castell Street.' This may be the house in Council Street, previously named School Lane, which house and farmyard have been held by the Stilgoe family under the Windsor Manor of Deddington since the early part of the 17th century and probably earlier. In the year 1917 it was enfranchised by the Copyholder Henry Edward Stilgoe and is now in occupation of D. Bliss as tenant."

A little further towards Clifton is that fine Jacobean house, formerly 'The Green', now known as the 'Poplars'. The date above the porch is 1647, and the un-modernized gabelled side is beautifully proportioned. The other has the appearance of having been added to, perhaps rebuilt after a fire. Christ Church College has lately sold it, but the white plastering characteristic of its property still remains. The house has a farm history, having been associated with the famous Appletree family. But for two generations, stretching over a period of 90 years, it was occupied by medical men, the Turners, father and son. Dr. Turner, the grandson, however, removed to a house on the Oxford Road.

Traditions die hard in Deddington. One that links the 'Green' or 'Poplars' with yet another medical memory must be taken for what it is worth, being some two hundred years old.

"In old Dr. Appletree's day (John Appletree, Apothecary, was granted a faculty for a seat in the Parish Church, December 17th, 1728), said Mr. Thomas Deeley, carrier, to me, "I've heard tell there was a ghost at the Poplars and they got the parson in to lay it."

Beauty is said to be in the eye ; certainly, judging from the following extract, there was none in that of the beholder who, in the earlier years of the reign of King George the third, recorded his impressions of our gold-brown town in Walpole's British Traveller.

'Doddington, or Deddington, is a place of great antiquity, and formerly sent members to Parliament ; but that privilege has been long taken away, though on what account is not known. It had anciently a castle, but not the least vestige of it now remains. It is at present a very poor town under the government of a bailiff ; and exclusive of a Charity School, has not a single building that merits particular notice. The weekly market is on Saturday, and the distance from London sixty-two miles.'

4. TRADES AND CALLINGS.

A decayed market town ! It is our village epitaph and sad as true. One by one its industries have left it, due partly to change of methods and demand, partly to much increased swiftness in transport, the last being the chief factor in making Banbury market and town the trading centre it now is. Horses, leather gaiters and other specialities, together with the famed pudding pies of Deddington Fair, are no longer in demand here, but several good shops still successfully ply for orders round about, as well as supplying the needs on the spot.

Change from horse power to petrol in the end did away with a very famous industry—Joseph and Samuel Mason's Axle-tree factory. Its last proprietor was John Ward who sold the patent to Walker's of Wednesbury. But such a hall-mark of excellence was Mason's of Deddington that other axle-trees used to arrive at their destination by a round-about route in order to get labelled with Deddington's nearest railroad equivalent. It was established about 1820 and removed 37 years ago. Some 60 to 80 men were employed at the foundry on whose former site the British Legion Club building now stands A member of the Clark family who worked there still survives, and Mrs. Robert Tucker, wife of the ex-postmaster (now retired and living at the "Priory", Hudson Street) is a daughter of its last Deddington proprietor, John Ward. It was the firm's proud boast that hardly a crowned head in Europe but rode in state above those axle-trees, and Queen Victoria's Coronation coach was furnished with them.

Most lamentable of all—perhaps because to the outsider it does not appear to have been inevitable in spite of war-time eclipse— was the closing down of Franklin's Church building and restoration firm.

The brothers H. Robert and W. Franklin carried out other work of a high class, but it was in connection with the embellishment and restoration of ecclesiastical buildings they were most noted. Mr. David Hancox, one of Franklin's head men, has been good enough to furnish a record of some of the work executed by the late H. R. and W. Franklin between 1884 and 1916—a formidable list though detailing only a part of their achievements. Space permits but a meagre selection from a range that includes every form of design and artistry in wood, stone and brickwork.

Of famous Churches and Schools, names that spring to the eye are St. Giles' and St. Margaret's, Oxford ; Cowley St. John's ; Stratford-on-Avon Church ; Magdalen College ; the Abbeys of Wroxall and Barton ; Marlborough College, Salisbury School and

Cripplegate, London ; Clumber, Eccleston, Burton-on-Trent, St. Ives. Franklin's range was not local but throughout the Kingdom and beyond it, for Hobart Cathedral, Tasmania, prizes among its greatest treasures a pulpit and chancel screen made by Deddington's artist-craftsmen, finished and transported thither, respectively in 1903 and 1916. Chancel screens were perhaps most in request. Franklin's specimens of oak carving and design up and down the country did not, however, by any means stop there. Pulpits, organ cases, rood beams, panelling, reredos, etc., alike gave scope to a skill for which the Deddington workshop served both as training school and headquarters of rare master builders, equipped for dealing with materials the most massive, intricacies the most delicate.

Mr. Hancox's list ends with words briefly tragical. '13th February, 1917, finished for Franklin's as works closed down.'

Thus was 'finis' written—a loss not only in employment to a couple of hundred (sometimes more) of the highly skilled, but to the community at large for whom that skill was no longer exercised.

....

'Aynho on the hill,
Clifton in the Clay,
Dirty, drunken Deddington
And Hempton high way.'

We may deprecate, we may smile, we may even try to explain away, but the fact remains that such is our local rhyme and we had better make the best of it.

'This town like Banbury has been long celebrated for the goodness of its malt liquor, from whence it obtained the appellation of *Drunken Deddington*', wrote the compiler of the 1852 Directory and Gazetteer of Oxfordshire. Malt was a principal product—maybe competitors were jealous, and anyway those who too well appreciated Deddington's beer no doubt came from far and wide to bring upon the town its bibulous reputation.

Notes from the Latin Roll of A.D. 1424, relate that at the Court held in 'Dadynton' the following officials were elected for the ensuing year :—

'One Bailiff, two constables, three Beer Tasters, three overseers of butchers and bakers, who are to report concerning false weight, or inferior quality.'

Severe penalties and punishments were in store for offenders, and we may note that the standard of beer had three to keep it up, while meat and bread shared three between them. Even so the liquor of Deddington has been well guarded right up to the days of John Knibbs, 'Ale Taster' by appointment of 'Court Leet' who tasted for the Bailiffs to see that the beer was up to standard. He died aged ninety-four on March the 9th, 1901. Knibbs also combined with this the Town criership, an office at present held by the sexton, who has now little occasion to ring his bell and proclaim.

In spite of belonging to another County (Northampton), Aynho plays an important part in local history besides heading the local rhyme. First, obstructing in 1858, through its Squire, Deddington's desire to become a poor law centre. Later, making amends by procuring a privilege. For Anyho's Squire—bargaining this time instead of obstructing—obtained for would-be travellers the boon of a second Great Western Railway Station, 'Aynho Park.' A shorter cut to London via Bicester having been devised, this was the condition exacted by Squire Cartwright for permission to run the line across his property.

Mr. David Hancox, whose hobby is bee-keeping, tells a story that again links Anyho-on-the-hill with the Deddington that drinks. It recalls the times when malt liquor as intoxicant had a formidable rival in the bee wine of antiquity. A man of Aynho brewed so much metheglin (fermented honey with the comb) that the Deddington and Aynho publicans did not like it. They caused his removal—by bribing or intimidation is not stated—so as to keep the coast clear for beer.

Bee-Master Hancox makes the more refined honey brew—mead. This, unlike metheglin, is fermented from the run honey without the comb and is a mellow, most insidious drink.
"I've got some in my cellar years old," said he, "it goes down like milk but when you've had a glass or two you know it !"

....

It has not been possible to get many particulars of weaving being carried on here though there is proof that cloth was made and sold. Mr. Henry Stilgoe calls attention to 'the Overseers' Accounts for the years 1736 and 1742, showing the labourers' wages, also where, or for whom, they worked. The fact that the Overseers sold cloth suggests that it was probably made by inmates of the institutions under their charge. There are entries which show that the cloth was sold at 7½d. and at 11d. per ell.'

An obstinate tradition, too, connects the plush weaving, still carried on at Shutford, with Deddington. The story goes that there were here weavers skilled in the art who left for the former place, possibly as a more convenient centre, it already being known for its plush. Judging from the pay and prices customary in the trade, which Beesley's History of Banbury (1841) quotes, its followers fared but hardly. Much plush was then exported from Banbury, (later on Shutford became headquarters of this class of weaving). It was in the style of velvet and looms were of the olden construction, the shuttles passed by hand as they still are. "A man," writes Beesley, "ought to make a piece of livery plush 42-43 yards in a month for which he would receive £3." Boys did the winding, earning on an average one shilling and tenpence halfpenny per week, and the weekly average earnings of the ordinary worker is put at eleven shillings and three farthings. They were at the looms for nine hours, six days a week.

Referring back to the local rhyme, 'Clifton in the Clay' held a fairly important place with its industries. 'Hempton high way' contributed nothing but the 'high way' mentioned, which was and is a good road for a healthful walk with beautiful views of the churches 'Adderbury for strength, Bloxham for length', though 'King's Sutton for beauty'—which completes another local rhyme —is not so clearly in the line of visibility.

At Clifton a beaver hat factory was run in conjunction (rather aptly !) with the 'Duke of Cumberland's Head' and was apparently a thriving concern, especially when a low crowned beaver was as an important part of the rustic's Sunday dress as his smock and ribbed stocking. These three items were insisted upon by William Hirons in his recollections of 80 and 90 years ago. Farming implements, pumps and agricultural machinery made by Thomas Lardner was another source of prosperity.

Robinson's mill at Clifton is the only one in the Deddington district still working. Formerly there were several, the mills of Clifton being especially mentioned as contributing to the revenues of the Prior of Bicester in 1425, the priors having been holders of one-third of the Manor of Deddington since 1272, when even then our mills were grinding to provide the daily bread.

Names enshrining memories of mills no longer there are the Windmill Cottages on the Hempton Road and Paper Mill Lane, turning out of the Banbury Road on the east side and running towards the small river Swere. John Emberlin (1791) carried on his business of paper-making here, and Sophia Emberlin (1846) was probably the last of the paper-makers of that name. Subsequently one Hobday occupied it, and in the 'eighteen-seventies' Z. W. Stilgoe of Adderbury Grounds purchased it and converted it to the purposes of a corn mill. Good writing paper, also Bank Note paper used to be made at these paper mills.

Going back to the annals of Deddington's traders, two names are conspicuous in the beginning and middle of the last century. William Hudson gave his name to a street and through his executors presented the Church clock. He was draper and storekeeper in Market Square where Wells & Son's furniture business is carried on: Centenarian Hirons with his characteristic chuckle told me, "Bill Hudson gave the Church clock—out of farthings they said ! He had a general shop, grocer's and drapers, at Chislett's Corner. One day he went to get out a teapot for a party he was giving and sovereigns began dropping out of it on to the floor. (Didn't trust banks much in those days, you know, so he'd hidden them there). 'Never mind', says Bill, 'a sovereign or two don't matter'," which displayed a latitude certainly not usually associated with farthing hoarding though in sympathy with the disposition which planned giving so fine a clock.

The other big name in those days was John Samuel Hiron, printer, bookbinder, bookseller and stationer ; he also sold music and Berlin wools. From his establishment in the Market Place he published "The North Oxfordshire Monthly Times." Its first number was issued on July 3rd, 1849 and it was continued until December 1859—possibly, according to Mr. Marshall, for a longer time. The newspaper was during the latter part of its career issued from Hiron's premises in the High Street. The sub-title of this publication was the "Agricultural Advertiser" and it appeared on the first Tuesday in each month. Mr. Thomas Smith, who has several copies of this journal, kindly lent them with much other valuable information on local history.

Naturally Mr. Hiron's advertising columns refer to his own 'special lines'. His was the 'Stamp Office' where licences—ranging from 'marriage' to 'hawkers' were sold. Among new songs to be obtained at Hiron's Music Warehouse were 'Oh, Willy we have missed you', 'Popping the Question', and 'Old Dog Tray.' Mr. Hiron also sold Horniman's tea and was a medicine vendor. Banbury tradesmen inserted their advertisements too in the 'Monthly Times', and a novelty recommended by one of these— 'patent elastic trouserings on an entirely new principle which for comfort and durability is unequalled'—makes one smile, though they were most likely far less absurd than the late 'Oxford bags'.

John and Thomas Fardon had the reputation for making excellent clocks here ; many examples of their work are still in use. Their names appear in a 'Universal Directory' published 1791-2. From this we also find that the King's Arms, kept by John Williams was, exactly one hundred and forty years ago, the Post Office. Thomas George and George Goodman were malsters—the old way of writing 'maltsters', William Williams a cooper, John Emberlin a paper-maker. The Fardons are described as watch-makers, Thomas being an iron-monger too. Thomas Williams kept the Three Tuns.

Under the heading of 'Traders etc.' are Jeremiah Knibbs, collar maker ; Richard Knibbs, Sadler ; Thomas Knibbs, Girt-weaver ; John Martin, peruke-maker, and William Skillman, School-master.

There was another innkeeper, who was a freeholder as well, Edmund French, but it does not give the name of his public house.

From Hunt and Co's Directory for 1846 the following names and callings are selected as throwing a light on the development of the place and its industries. Foremost, the axle-tree makers— Mason, Joseph and Samuel (patent). Auctioneer and Appraiser, Scroggs, John (the name of the last is noteworthy, for as Mr. Marshall in his Notes observes, he represented the family of Sir William Scroggs, Chief Justice in 1678, a Deddingtonian who rose to high office from humble parentage).

The Beer Retailers were W. Heritage, G. E. Petty, John Timms and George Whetton. Hop Merchants : Edward Bradley and William Margetts. John Samuel Hirons is set down as 'Bookseller and Stationer, Printer and Binder'. The King's Arms was kept by Ann East, it was 'Commercial and Posting'. The Unicorn, by William Sturch, was 'Commercial.' Inns and Public Houses were the Crown and Tuns, George Morrey ; King's Head,. Thomas Rutter ; Plough, Thomas Matthews ; Red Lion, John Rose ; Three Horse Shoes, John Whetton.

Malsters were two : G. E. Petty, who figured previously as beer-retailer, and John Scroggs, unexpectedly combining malt with his auctioneering. Five straw hat makers are enumerated, it was a home occupation for women. Three 'Hannahs', respectively Ford, Franklin and Nutt, made hats, as did Elizabeth Strong and Mary Town.

Sophia Emberlin (in Hunt's Directory mis-spelt 'Embling') was carrying on the paper making, and there were no fewer than five Fire and Life Assurance Agents, who witnessed to the rapid popularity of that admirable and prudential safeguard.

By 1852—the date of both the Kelly's Post Office Directory and the Oxfordshire Gazetteer, to which reference is frequently made—family names had changed less than businesses, though even these often have remained the same up to this day. There are Bennetts, one a baker, who we know made pudding pies. There are two John Bakers, Senior and Junior, both connected with the building trade. Four Hopcrafts made bricks, were masons, potters or stone-cutters. The famous Robert Franklin, under heading 'builder' is in the list. There are many named Churchill, Busby, Gibbs, French, Smith—all pursuing callings necessary to the community and several combining more than one.

For instance, George Eustace Petty was a brewer and malster who retailed his beer besides selling china, corn and coal. William Matthews, whose rope-walk was behind Hopcraft's building yard, made rope and hair-line. There were makers of bonnets and a maker of clogs, and the keepers of a 'Seminary', and 'Academy', and a 'Dame's School', commented upon elsewhere. Needless to say the farmers and agricultural interests were of immense importance but their place is not in a trade list. Also it goes without saying that their names, if enumerated, would closely repeat those farming today. As a stranger said to Mr. Thomas Smith, who was explaining a little about us—

"Why, good gracious me, the whole of Deddington seems to be related."

So much bustling activity in this market town, which is now a village, necessitated naturally plenty of means of transport for goods and for those passengers not catered for by the flying coaches.

Carrier services between Deddington and Oxford, and the towns of Banbury and Woodstock were as follows :—

To Banbury : Richard French, Mondays, Thursdays and Saturdays ; Joseph Hemmings, Mondays and Thursdays ; Thomas Gibbard, every Saturday ; Thomas Nutt, (from Milton) every Thursday.

To Oxford : Joseph Hemmings, every Wednesday and Saturday ; Thomas Gibbard, every Saturday ; Thomas Nutt, (from Milton) every Friday.

To Woodstock : Johnson and Ward from the Unicorn, Tuesdays, Thursdays and Saturdays.

London was reached through Parker's vans from the King's Arms every Tuesday and Saturday. They passed through Aynho and Bicester to Aylesbury where they joined the train.

To post a letter to London from Deddington in 1826 cost eightpence. (Vide Paterson's Roads).

5. DEDDINGTON FOLK.

PART I.

Apart from interest in Deddington's manorial rights the town has been singularly free from the protection or over-shadowing of any royal or noble house. It produced, however, many good specimens of the classes called 'the backbone of England'—yeomen, traders and professional men. It had, too, distinguished men, and of these without doubt the greatest born here was Sir Thomas Pope.

'He rose to a position of great wealth and influence under Henry the eighth and his successors', remarks Mr. Griggs in 'Highways and Byways in Oxford and the Cotswolds', and he goes on to quote Aubrey who mentions that 'he could have rode in his owne lands from Coggs (by Witney) to Banbury about 18 miles.' A clear and authoritative account of his rise and origin is given briefly by the Rev. E. Marshall in his 'Notes' as follows :—

'The family to which he (Thomas Pope) belonged was settled in Kent in the reign of Edward III, where it held a respectable position. A branch of it is found soon after this in Deddington, where John and Margaret Pope were living in 1401. William Pope of Deddington, who was probably a lineal descendant of these, was the father of Sir Thomas Pope. He possessed land in Deddington, and died in 1523, leaving his estate to his wife for her widowhood, with remainder to his son Thomas, who was a minor of about the age of fourteen, and for whom he otherwise made provision by his will. Every care appears to have been taken of his education. He was sent to the school at Banbury and to Eton College. He then became a member of Gray's Inn, and in due time an eminent lawyer. He held several important offices under the Crown, and was made by the King, Treasurer of the Court of Augmentations, under which came the administration of the revenues arising from the dissolution of the monasteries. He obtained, as Thomas Pope, of Dodyngton, Esq., the following grant of arms in 1535 : "Party per pale or and azure, on a chevron between three gryphons' heads erased four fleur-de-lis all counterchanged," and was knighted the following year. He was the founder of Trinity College, Oxford, in 1555. The custody of the lady (afterwards Queen) Elizabeth at Hatfield was entrusted to him for the four last years of Mary's life. His death took place at his house at Clerkenwell on January 29, 1558-9, in the fiftieth year of his age. He was buried at St. Stephen's, Walbrook, in the vault where his wife Margaret and his daughter Alice had previously been buried......

But in 1567 the bodies of Sir Thomas Pope and his wife were removed to the Chapel of Trinity College and re-interred, where a large tomb, with recumbent figures of himself and his third wife Elizabeth, was placed with this inscription :—

"Hic jacent corpora Thome Pope militis Fundatoris hujus Collegii Trinitatis et domine Elizabethe et Margarite Uxoris ejus ; qui quidem Thome obit XXIX die Januarii MDLVIII."

"Quod Tacitum Velis Nemini Dixeris," which admirable motto Mr. Marshall translates thus :—"What e'er you wish untold, to no one tell."

Beautifully sculptured in alabaster, the woodwork so elaborately carved by Grinling Gibbons (1691) is cut away to reveal it. Oil paintings of himself in ermine bordered robes, and his wife (Lady Elizabeth Paulet) in a rich dress with velvet sleeves and head-dress sewn with pearls, hang over the mantel in the Commons room. Sir Thomas is also the subject of a stone bust in a niche of the outside wall. Quite recently Trinity College has gladly paid the sum of three hundred pounds for a drawing of their founder taken from life.

'The Visitation of the County of Oxford' 1574 records that John and Margaret Pope were commemorated on a window of Deddington Church, with their two children. Simply the names and dates, without any coat of arms, that being conferred on their eminent descendant. This is the entry :—

"John (Pope) et Margreata uxor ejus & Gaverell (Gabriel) and Anne his children wch Margret died the last of August MCCCI William Pope and Julian and Margret his wiffes wch W dessessed the XXVth of Marche Mdxxiii." 'W' of course stands for William.

The poet Alexander Pope described himself as descended from a family in Oxfordshire, the head of which was the Earl of Downe. As the first Earl of Downe was Sir William Pope, nephew of the founder of Trinity College, this brings the poet into the line of Deddington ancestry. Lord Downe, too, in 1618, built Wroxton Abbey, the seat of the Norths, into whose family the lease was carried by his grand-daughter and heiress, the house still remainng the property of Trinity College. The last Prior of Wroxton had subscribed to the Royal Supremacy and in this manner the Estate had passed into the hands of Sir Thomas Pope. The Lee-Dillons also have a place in the Pope descent as sketched by Mr. **Marshall.**

Treasurer of the Court of Augmentation is the high office stressed on Sir Thomas Pope's memorial inscription, and when it is remembered his duty was to go into facts and accounts bearing on the dissolution of religious enstablishments with income of less than £200 yearly, it was matter for congratulation, doubtless, that the head investigator was of such good repute. The Priory of Bicester, not having the required income, was dissolved by an earlier Act of Henry VIII passed in 1536. 'In the following year,' states Mr. Marshall, 'the manor of Deddington, "late of the monastery of Bicester", was granted by the king to Sir Thomas Pope. In 1545 this was again in the possession of the king, having been re-purchased by him of Sir Thomas Pope. It was subsequently conveyed by him to the Cathedral of Christ Church, as "the manor of Deddington, late of Sir Thomas Pope, in the king's hand by purchase."

The Oxfordshire Archaeological Society's report for 1930, quotes from the 'Surrender and Pension list of November 17th, 1539 (Dissolution of Religious Houses with less annual income than £200) that 'Juliana Pope (alias Deddington), Benedictine nun of Godstowe' had a pension of £6.13.4. assigned to her, and she was still on the pension list in 1556.

Sir William Scroggs, the other great lawyer of Deddington, has left a less fragrant memory. A short biographical account is given of him in Marshall's 'Notes.'

'In 1623, there was born at Deddington, of parents belonging to the town, one who rose to a high place, but of whom Bishop Burnet observes, in the *History of his own Time*, that he was "a man more valued for a good readiness in speaking well, than either for learning in his profession, or for any moral virtue." Sir William Scroggs, who became Chief-Justice in 1678, was first at Oriel and Pembroke Colleges, and took his degree as M.A., and afterwards became an officer in the King's Services. He was originally intended for holy orders, but he entered upon the study of the law as a member of Gray's Inn, and at length obtained the post just mentioned. While he was at the head of the King's Bench, the trials of the supposed conspirators in the Popish Plot took place. In the first year's trials at which he presided, to use again an expression of Bishop Burnet, "he set himself, even with indecent earnestness, to get the prisoners to be always cast." But in the second year when the queen's interests were at stake, at the trial of Wakeman and the three priests, "he summed up very favourably for the prisoners, contrary to his former practice." In 1680 he was impeached by the Commons for high treason ; but the matters alleged against him were only misdemeanours, and the impeachment was rejected...The following year, however, he was dismissed from his high office ; after which he retired to his estate at Weald Hall, near Brentwood, in Essex, where he died in 1683......The family of Scroggs (written 1879) is represented in Deddington by Mr. John Scroggs, of the Horsefair.'

A painting of Sir William Scroggs is in the National Portrait Gallery of London.

The Oxfordshire Gazetteer (1852) says of Scroggs—'his father was a tradesman in the town and is by some said to have been a butcher.' It quotes Dean Swift's verdict of Scroggs, which was severe :—"I have read somewhere of an Eastern king who put a judge to death for an iniquitous sentence, and ordered his hide to be stuffed into a cushion, and placed upon the tribunal for the son to sit on, who was preferred to the father's office. I fancy such a memorial might not have been useless to a son of Sir William Scroggs, and both he and his successors would often wriggle in their seats as long as the cushion lasted."

Lawyers seemed to have flourished in the place, several practising at one time as evidenced by the directories. In 1791-2 under heading 'Attorneys' are John Appletree, Samuel Churchill and Thomas Fidkin. Hants Directory for 1846 gives the names of John Churchill, Samuel Field, William Henry Hitchcock and John Francis Lamb. In 1852 all these are still in business with the exception of J. F. Lamb and the addition of C. Duffell Faulkner and one Kinch, taken into partnership by W. H. Hitchcock.

Coroner Churchill lived in New Street at Ilbury House ; lawyers otherwise lived by preference, when they could, at the Hermitage, Market Square, which was of course very central. Mr. Samuel Field, clerk to the magistrates of North Wootton Hundred, is still remembered by Mr. Thomas Smith (of Messrs. Stockton, Sons and Fortescue whose offices are opposite) as a very legal figure issuing in dignified manner from its doorway. Lawyer Kinch resided first in the Manor Farm (since rebuilt) and afterwards at the Hermitage, where Lawyer Coggins lived later. Mr. C. Duffell Faulkner, Solicitor, dwelt first at 'Gegg's Hook' by Deddington cross roads, and then removed to Hudson's Lane, named it is true after the Hudson who gave the church clock, but ever famous for Faulkner's residence and museum at 'the Priory' which he rebuilt.

As antiquarian and collector he earns respectful comment from contemporary writers. The museum of local curiosities which he collected—pre-historic and of every period—were on show in the roomy upper part of the house to which admission was free, Mr. Faulkner having no other object but to interest others in his valuable hobby. At his death the collection was dispersed to various London museums, but some fine fossils—notably a huge ammonite—gargoyles and other relics, still adorn the little garden and grotto opposite his old house, which also contains inside and out, various small sculptures, from angels to grotesques, evidence of his ruling passion.

Law is early linked with education in Deddington by the proposal of Sir Thomas Pope to establish a School. Marshall quotes an agreement with Trinity College, dated 1555, relating to the intended foundation of a free Grammar School, stating that "The said president, fellowes and schollers, shall yerely for evermore give and pay unto one hable person, well and sufficiently lerned and instructed in gramer and humanitie, which shall be *Schole Master* of and at a frescole, to be called *Jhesus Scole*, of the foundation of the said Sir Thomas Pope, to be erected at Dedington in the said countie of Oxon, and to teach children gramer and humanitie there frely, for his yerely salarye and wages XX marks, of good and lawfull money ; and to one other hable and lerned person in gramer to be *Usher* within the said frescole yerely viij of good and lawfull money, to teache children likewise ther frely."

But before giving prominence to any teacher who was appointed in consequence of Sir Thomas Pope's admirable plan, space must be afforded to the name of one previously in office. "The Countie of Oxford Certificate" drawn up by Edward the sixth's (1547-1553) Commissioners, in the following extract pays a warm tribute to a school-master who must surely have been known to Pope and perhaps inspired him to give such a man and his pupils better opportunities.

"Deddington
Ducastus Lancastrie.
"The late Guild of the Trynytie in the Parishe
Church of Dadyngton.
Houseling people 300.
William Burton, Incumbent there, hath for his salary, the tenth deducted £6, (The clere yerely valewe) £7.18s.10d., over and above all charges.

A scole there, the said William burton, Scolemaster.

The Towne of Dadyngton is parcell of the Duchie of Lancastre. The said William Burton ys a good scole master and Bryngyth up yough very well in learnyng."

From the Parish register of the period we learn that "on February 15th, 1672, the School-house was made in the church for Edward Kempster to teach theire."

In 1654, Edward Kempster was appointed "Registrar of the Parish," and Parish clerk in 1658. According to his memorial on the outside of the south wall of the church, which is rapidly decaying and much obliterated, the date of death in 1675, but the register contains the entry of his burial in the summer of 1676.

The inscription can be only partially deciphered. In 1879 the Rev. E. Marshall found it 'much worn' and naturally as years go by it can be read less and less. Mr. Henry Stilgoe deciphers it thus :—

"Near to this (stone ?)
Lyes ye body of
Edward Kempster
who dyed July ye 29
1675
............Kempster
Dyed Octob......
17   1724
Margery Kempster
(wh ?)o Dyed Sept ye 13
......8 aged 69
years."

The tablet is surmounted by a Cherub's head, and decorated with conventional foliage and flowers. The weather has caused the stone to flake off. E. Kempster's intelligent and conscientious annotations and entries in the registers add greatly to their value.

It is good to know that these two early school-masters—Burton and Kempster—were already upholding what has become a fine tradition. Few personal memories, however, survive of a succession of useful men, till the respected name of Thomas Alexander Manchip is reached. As the tablet placed in the chancel of the parish church 'in affectionate and grateful appreciation' sets forth, he was for 37 years headmaster of Deddington and for 34 years choirmaster. He died March 9th, 1911, aged 68. To Mr. Manchip's historical notes on Deddington this narrative is greatly indebted. And we may well rejoice that in Mr. John Harmsworth the children have a schoolmaster who has their welfare truly at heart.

Going back just over 200 years in our educational history an extract from the Magna Britannia, 1730, quoted by the Rev. E. Marshall, shows it proceeding then on a very small scale. There was at the time "A School for 16 boys and as many girls who are taught to read and say their Catechism at a penny a week per head, at the expense of a private gentleman."

'But more than this was required', writes Mr. Marshall. 'The Deddington National School Society was established on July 26th, 1814, and in October a School with 40 boys from Deddington and the neighbouring villages was opened with Mr. Thomas Osborne for its master, and a school for 40 girls with Miss Lucy Lee as mistress......'

Mr. William Cartwright conveyed the present site of 3 roods in 1853, and the Schools were opened in the beginning of 1854. But according to the 'North Oxfordshire Monthly Times,' published in Deddington, dated Dec. 4th, 1855, education here was soon in difficulty. For a letter printed therein laments that "a little over twelve months, after being in full operation under excellent teachers, first the boys School was closed ! And in June last year the girls' School shut up also !"

In this 'altered state of Church matters', an appeal is made to former subscribers to remedy 'such a deplorable state of things.' However in the issue of March 4th, 1856, a Deed (deposited in the Church Chest) is detailed, being one designed to correct what the previous writer describes 'as the gross mis-application of the Feoffee Charities' with special reference to 'the deplorable closing of Deddington Schools.'

....

If lawyers loomed largest, hard on them in importance followed the physicians and barber-surgeons, some of whom were of high repute. The first mention of a Deddington surgeon is found in the Oxford Marriage Bonds :—

'William Griffin, surgeon, 27 March 1677.'

Samuel Belchier, whose rather florid memorial in the Lady Chapel of the parish church records his death on December 9th, 1688, issued a trading token. It is described by Mr. W. Boyne (Marshall's Notes) as being one of four tradesmen's tokens circulating in Deddington, patents for them being authorized owing to the great scarcity of copper money. Those issuing them may safely be reckoned as notable business people. They were as follows :—

(1) Obverse : Samuel Belchier. 1688 ; centre : The Apothecaries' Arms.
Reverse : In.Dedington ; centre : His half peny. S.B.B.

(2) Obv. : John Elkington ; centre : A flying horse.
Rev. : In Dedington.1667 ; centre : His half peny.

(3) Obv. : Ann. Makepace. In ; centre : An eagle and child.
Rev : Dadington.Mercer ; centre : A.M. (farthing).

(4) Obv. : Thomas.Nutt.of ; centre : T.N.
Rev. : Dadington.Mercer ; centre : 1553. (farthing).

All except Ann Makepace, Mercer, state the date, but the period of Nutt's coin is earlier than Belchier's and Elkington's. being that of Queen Mary's Accession. The Nutt family vault is also in the Lady Chapel.

Another Belchier commemorated near by Samuel is the wife of Thomas Belchier, who died in 1718. John Appletree of Deddington, Apothecary, belonged to a notable family here. And a medical member of the Lane family, whose coat of arms and crest are sculptured on the outer south wall of the church has, inscribed on the flat stone of his grave immediately beneath, this tribute to one who was doubtless a noble follower of a noble profession :—

"Sacred
To the Memory of
John Lane
Who was both a Skilful Surgeon and
a benevolent man
who died 1736
Aged 68.

———

Our Saviour Jesus Christ both abolished
death and brought life and
immortality to light
by the Gospel."

———

The John and Francis Lane of Clifton mentioned in a Deed of Sale (1635) of land in Southampton, were this good doctor's ancestors.

Barbers remain—there are two barber's poles in Deddington, but the significance of their twisted pattern, meaning blood and bandages, has passed. One of the last of that old school of apothecaries, who combined a certain exercise of surgery with dispensing, was Mr. J. H. Smith who 80 years ago advertised himself by a neat professional card with ornamented edge. It runs :—

'J. H. Smith,
(Son of the late George Smith, Surgeon)
Chemist and Druggist, Deddington.
Physicians' prescriptions carefully dispensed.
Bleeding, Teeth extracted, and Cupping.'

Cupping was the application of glass cups from which the air had been exhausted to a scarified part of the skin, thus drawing blood. Some people submitted themselves to this operation periodically. Mr. J. H. Smith was a great-uncle of Miss Smith, Hon. Sec. to the Deddington Women's Institute.

The decline in church-going is too marked today for the shrinkage in congregations to be ascribed to a change from compulsion to convention. Yet that description would have been a fairly accurate one for half a century previous to the Great War. In pre-reformation days laymen had to produce proofs of observance of religious duties or go before the Bishop's Bench. And later attendance at divine worship was expected of everyone, and good behaviour too of juveniles or a rap from the beadle's staff. Conviction alone now is our compelling power.

But every now and then in every age, preachers of eloquence and magnetism fill big buildings. Such attractions caused a gallery to be added to Deddington parish church. Wing's Supplement to Marshall's Deddington tells us all about it.

'It was in 1822......Vicar Faulkner died and was succeeded by the Rev. Richard Greaves ; the present writer (born in 1810) well recollects the Rev. John Faulkner in the reading desk facing north with a clerk's seat below and a pulpit above, the whole forming a regular *three-decker*.'

'Mr. Greaves soon made a great name by preaching the opinions called Evangelical, so that Deddington church was filled Sunday after Sunday with people who admired Calvinistic doctrine, from all the surrounding villages, but the celebrity of Mr. Greaves was eclipsed by that of the curate he engaged, the Rev. John Hughes, who had previously been at Foleshill near Coventry. Though Deddington is 17 miles from Oxford, undergraduates would occasionally come on Sunday mornings to hear Greaves or Hughes.

The son and biographer of the latter states that the newly-made Cardinal, John Henry Newman, was among those excursionizing undergrads at least once. Mr. Hughes had the misfortune to be left a widower with six young children, the eldest under nine years, while he was curate of Deddington, where we believe he effected many useful reforms. Shortly after his crushing bereavement he became Incumbent of Aberystwyth and Vicar of Llanbadarn Fawr, and eventually Archdeacon of Cardigan, and he died in 1860, to the last an attached member and servant of the National Church. Not so his superior, the Rev. Richard Greaves, who soon after he resigned Deddington forsook the Church wherein he had been baptized and ordained, and joined those who are said to hold Unitarian doctrine.'

In was during his vicariate that William Hudson's clock was added to the church.

Horse-box pews were provocative of naps, and the three-decker combined pulpit, reading desk and clerk's stall had on one occasion that has been handed down, somewhat the same influence —intensified by a too prolonged visit between services to the Red Lion. A certain vicar whose failings were those of an age, happily past, slept so soundly in his desk that the congregation departed.

"They're all gone," said the clerk, finally rousing him.

"All gone ?" said the sleepy parson, "well, fill 'em up again !"

5. DEDDINGTON FOLK.

PART II.

What's in a name ? Often a great deal of history, a clue to the occupation or residence of the first head of a family to be known by it. But the nearer to this source of information, that is the longer ago, the more indifferent were people as to the spelling of it. After the Norman names of those barons, on whom or their descendants kings bestowed territorial possessions, the earliest our history records are quite humble-sounding trade names, though fantastically abbreviated. We were under the jurisdiction of the Prior of Burcestre (Bicester), a gift of one-third of Deddington Manor made by Gilbert Bassett in 1272, giving the right to try felons, and the assize of bread and beer.

The following note from the Latin Rolls (kept at the Record Office, Chancery Lane, London) dated Michaelmas, A.D. 1424, in the reign of Henry VI, begins thus :—

'The jury say that Thomas Skynne (Skinner) holds ten acres of land in Dadyngton which formerly belonged to Thomas Drap (Draper)......'

The names of the jury are Thomas Yereman, Will Wyghthull, Will Hokard (Awkward), John Somerton.

Mr. H. E. Stilgoe, who supplied the extracts from the Latin Rolls where quoted, remarks on the prevalence of the names Thomas, William and John in those times. One can match this with almost as great a popularity for the name Samuel in the beginning of the 19th and latter end of the 18th centuries. Some names in the early records are illegible, others have to be elucidated. Such are 'Herreyes' for 'Harris' and 'Yremonghere' for 'Ironmonger.'

John Billing, Gent., December 1st, 1547, is another early entry under heading 'Dadington Manor and Rectory, Oxfordshire.' To him was granted 'the scite of the Castle, Dadington, for 21 years at 50s.' A near relative, perhaps son of the wool merchant William Byllyng who died in 1533. Copied from the Visitation of Oxford A.D.1574 is the description of an 'Askochen' (escutcheon) in Mr. Byllyng's house. The spelling of the surname is a blend of both, but the date puts it at considerable distance from the first Byllyng's death. He was probably content with the emblem of a *bill* through the body of a *ling* which the Red Lion Inn once bore upon its door.

— 56 —

The first of the Harris family spelt 'Herreyes' had plenty of his name to follow, and later members were distinguished. Mr. H. E. Stilgoe remarks :—

'The names of William Bindon Blood and John Hyde Harris in the 1846 Directory call for particular notice. The former reminds one of the distinguished General of that name, and of the Liverpool family of Blood.

'John Hyde Harris lived in the Market Square, Deddington. Carved upon the stone mantel-piece in a room of his house will be found the Harris family coat of arms, three hedgehogs, as on the monument upon the south wall of the church. He was the grandson of John Harris and Mary his wife, daughter of Nathaniel Stilgoe of Deddington. John Hyde Harris died 24th July, 1886, at Dunedin, Otago, New Zealand, aged 60 years. He was a barrister-at-law and held an official position there.' His house now belongs to Mr. H. Wells. It used to be called the Grange.

In the Roll of Quit Rents for June 1710 is a Thomas Makepeace (surely a descendant of Ann Makepeace, Mercer, who issued a money token) living in 'a house called the Bell.' There are no Billings or Makepeaces now, and a name much more recently important, long associated with the place has also disappeared from the neighbourhood.

This is 'Appultree,' 'Appletree', later 'Apletree'. A lease from the Dean and Canons of the free royal chapel of St. George, Windsor, brings in the famous name of Pope together with that of 'Appultree,' so spelt when first we meet it. It reads—'to Thomas Pope of Dadyngton in the county of Oxon., gentleman, and Thomas Appultree of Dadyngton of the Rectory of Dadyngton, presentation excepted, for 20 years, rent thirty-two pounds and a pension to the Vicar of 25 marks. To have the usual livery of 6/8. Signed by Thomas Pope and mark of Thomas Appultree. 20 June 1528. Seal.'

'Livery' here would mean 'delivered' in a legal sense. The Vicar's 'marks' were coins worth 13/4 each, but possessing far greater spending power then than a present-day equivalent would.

The connection of both Pope and Appultree families with the Rectory is interesting, for the great Sir Thomas Pope is reputed to have been born at the 'Rectorial Farmhouse', which of course could well have been occupied by his father, William Pope, irrespective of the rectorial rights. Apletree's too, were evidently associated with that house, though their home for generations was 'the Green' (Poplars).

A lease in the Court Rolls immediately after that to which Thomas Appultree set his mark, is one from an Adderbury man (John Bustard) 'of lands in Dadyngton recently purchased by him of Thomas Pope, and also his moiety of the Parsonage, tythe and demesne lands of the Parsonage and also of the domination or lordship of the Dean and Chapter of Windsor, and a tenement of the Dean and Chapter's called Leaden Porch, for 21 years, rent £11 and to pay the usual pension to the Vicar. Signed by John Edmunds, 20 December, 1534.'

The same Court Rolls record in 1615 '24 papers in the suit between the Dean and Canons of Windsor v. Thomas Appletree and others concerning the rectory, castle and Park of Dadington. They are 'Appletrees' too, in 1661, when Thomas Appletree, father and son, lease Leaden Porch from the Windsor Manor. But the family name is 'Apletree' when Nathaniel Apletree as steward to the Dean and Chapter, puts his signature on June 14th 1710, as having examined particulars and accounts in the Survey of Windsor Manor in 'Dadington'.

William Wing in his 'Supplement' writes 'at this period (beginning of 19th century) the Apletree family continued to reside in Deddington as they had done for many generations—we find one of them alluded to in a sneering entry in the North Aston Register of Marriages *"as a very great man in Deddington."* At the same time one Richard Apletree created a rent charge of 6s. & 8d. yearly on two acres of meadowland towards the maintenance of the north aisle of the Church.' In 1618 William Apletree formed a body of trustees for the public charities, one result of which was the erection and endowment of Almshouses.

The last representative of the family here was the Miss Apletree who married Simpson, the last farmer of the Castle House. She was humorously called 'the last of the appletrees.'

THE STILGOE FAMILY.

The opportunity of studying a family that in one branch has been 'under observation', so to say, in our parish as landowners and cultivators of the land for just over four hundred years is most interestingly afforded by the Stilgoes. Mr. Henry Edward Stilgoe, C.B.E., F.S.A., besides drawing information from the many documents in his possession has delved deep into historical records, and the result is a close acquaintance with a yeoman stock, which reaching out in divers directions touches national life at various points.

For the purpose of this narrative Mr. Stilgoe has very kindly allowed access to his notes from which the following brief account is summarised.

The surname is an early one of origin unknown, but names ending in 'oe' are said to be of Danish origin. Tracing back to the first mentions of it found obtainable, a John Stillego in the County of Worcester was one of the inquisitors at a post mortem on 11th April 1280. In Patent Roll 4 Edw.III (1330-1) Johanne Stilligo is termed Chamberlain to Queen Isabella (Queen of Edw. II.) and granted the custody of the Castle and gaol of Eye in Suffolk, and in the 6th year of Edward III's reign he receives a pardon for the escape of a prisoner, signed by the king at York.

In 1332-6 there is an agreement concerning land in the neighbourhood of Brentford, Ealing and Isleworth in names of John Stillego and Agatha his wife. And six years later in the Patent Rolls, 12 Edw.III, Agatha Stilligo is granted '4½d per day during the time the King is in foreign parts, she being too infirm to accompany him.'

There is documentary evidence that the family—or a branch of it—has been resident at Deddington since the year 1531, and its members have been copyholders under the Deddington Manors, also freeholders there since the 16th century and probably earlier.

In the report of the Oxfordshire Archaeological Society for 1930, the Rev. H. Salter contributes an article on a Visitation recorded in a volume at Lincoln Cathedral dated 1540, two years before Deddington was removed from that diocese by Henry VIII's foundation of the bishopric of Oxford. He quotes various interesting extracts and the following headed 'Deddington deanery ; in the church there,' is translated from the Latin.

'James Brooke has frequented and still frequents the company of the wife of Richard Perkins, in spite of many monitions from his neighbours. He denied the charge and on 11 October (1540) at Chippingnorton produced Thomas Brown and Richard Stilgoo, with whom he took oath and purged himself. The judge warned him,' etc.

Thus bringing from yet another source a Stilgoe into our history.

Documentary evidence again proves that there were Stilgoes in London and in Shropshire in the 16th century. But the London Stilgoes were those linked with Deddington—unexpectedly, for their interests were those of the sea and ships. Humphrey Stilgo, (son of the Humphrey who took up his freedom as a Cloth-worker in 1567), was a shipbuilder of New Gravel Lane, Stepney, and his son, Jeremy, was captain of "the good ship Rebecca." Jeremy Stilgoe had a son Zachary, who was captain of the "Ruby" (in the East India Company's service), and the name of Zachary, or Zachariah, in conjunction with Stilgoe, rings familiarly in Deddington ears, for it is deeply associated, through several bearers of it, with local history.

Mr. H. E. Stilgoe remarks that the troublous times of the 16th and 17th centuries, what with Civil War and Plague, wrought havoc in the lives of people. Many emigrated and records are difficult to trace. However in 1635 two Deddington names occur. One Ann Waterman, connected with this place, is in a list of emigrants to Virginia by the ship "Safety," August 1635. And Anthony Stilgoe also sails from the Port of London to Virginia, (July 24th, 1635) on the "Assurance." Richard the brother of this Anthony Stilgoe it is who is the connecting link between those Londoners, seafarers and shipbuilders, and the Deddington family whose interests were so essentially of the land, for in the year 1616 he was apprenticed to Humphrey Stilgoe, citizen and clothworker of London. He was a son of Thomas Stilgoe of "Dadington" who died in 1615, and Thomas's father was Anthony Stilgoe, described as a 'husbandman,' whose Will, made in 1606, is so characteristic of the yeoman of his day that the copy of it in the appendix will be found interesting reading.

The Deddington Parish Registers not commencing until the year 1631, earlier information from that source is unobtainable. The burial of a Zachary Stilgoe is recorded there in 1669, and that of his wife Mary in 1651. He left property here to his son Hugh, and directly from that line the present family of Stilgoes are descended. From the list of Quit Rents given at a Presentment of the Court Baron held on June 14th, 1710, the Zachary Stilgoe of that day appears to have been the principal leaseholder, having the

Parsonage House and Garden and
The Vicarage Garden   £10.
The Great Fishurie   £24.
(held jointly with Nathaniel Parsons).
The Castle   £10.

And 'Zackariah Stilgoe' is quoted in the same as paying the nominal sum of 6d. 'for a Freehold house called Stony House'.

He was a Malster.

Another Zachariah farmed at Blakesley, and subsequently at Maidford, building Maidford Grange. He died in 1831 and is buried with his wife in Deddington Church. Their son—the first to be christened 'Zachariah Walden'—died in 1823, aged only 25 ; he is also with the Zachariah Walden Stilgoe (1829-1878) of the Grounds, Adderbury, commemorated near by in the Parish Church.

Apropos of these Zachariahs there is an interesting relic in the possession of the family, which shows the name was prized. It is a brass tobacco box, engraved on one side with the Stilgoe family Coat of Arms, the initials 'Z.S.' one letter on either side of the Crest, and the date 1668. On the other side of the box is engraved the legend, 'This box is bequeathed to him whose name is Zach : Stilgoe for ever.'

The Coat of Arms (Fox Davies' "Armorial Families") is—Argent, a chevron gules, cottised gules, between three falchions (or cutlasses), proper.

Crest—a dexter arm bare, tied with a ribbon gules, holding a falchion, proper. Motto, Male mori quam foedari."

The Zakariah who died in 1831 had a son, Nathaniel Stilgoe. Nathaniel lived in Deddington, during the latter part of his life in the house in Council Street now owned by Mr. W. J. French. He died there in 1867. A picture of him with his servant Thomas Hayward, photographed from a sepia drawing by Joseph Wilkins of Deddington, shows him on horseback, with Deddington Church tower in the distance. Nathaniel Stilgoe is depicted in the typical dress of the period, which would be blue coat with gilt buttons, chamois leather colour waistcoat, silk hat, etc.

Henry, brother of this Nathaniel, had Plummer's Furse, Evenley, a farm of 499 acres, but left there in 1830, and went to Adderbury Grounds where he died. This farm is now occupied by Mr. Hugh William Stilgoe, J.P., brother to Mr. Henry Edward Stilgoe. It has been continuously in the occupation of the family since 1830.

6. DEDDINGTON FAIRS.

THE PUDDING PIE FAIR.

Deddington fairs are given in the 'History, Gazetteer and Directory of the County of Oxford (1852)" as August 10th, the Saturday after Old Michaelmas and November 22nd. The last was the "pudding pie Fair" and its glory over-shadowed all the rest. Weather lore has been associated with it from time immemorial.

'What the wind is at midnight 'fore Deddington Fair, so will it mostly stay the rest of the year.' "Or for three months ahead," said Mr. William Hirons, Deddington's oldest inhabitant ; "I noticed the wind blowing right from Duns Tew this last fair day (1931) and South-West its been mostly since."

That was spoken in January 1932, Mr. Hirons being then almost certainly well over one hundred years of age, for he distinctly remembered *walking* to his baptism, which is registered 98 years ago. He was a shining example of the adage that hard work never kills, and to his exact and lively memory this record owes much.

"Four o'clock in the morning and a fine day for the pudding pie Fair !" That was how the Watchman ushered it in. If it were not fine one wonders whether he had the heart to say so ! Wet or dry anyhow there were pudding pies, and buying and selling and much noise.

The Fair figures yet in the list and is fitfully, very slightly in evidence. In 1931 quite thirty young cart horses and Welsh ponies were trotted out for sale along the 'Horse Fair' ; the ponies, pretty wild creatures in their rough coats, travelling with their drovers through likely counties where there might be a chance to dispose of them before beginning the expense of winter feed.

Previously for quite two years there had been no sign of horsedealing, merely the rather pathetic sight of a dozen donkeys with the traditional high pommels and pinafore covers, brought into the market place under the assumption that the school children would have a holiday, which they did not. However, as the donkeys were ascertained to be on their way to winter quarters in Wales after a strenuous seaside season, lack of patronage was no grief to them.

Pudding pies have not been made in Deddington for the past six years. Miss Ruth Fowler of "the Old Bakery", whose family had the original recipe from the Bennetts, who were baking in 1852, undoubtedly made that historic delicacy just as it should be, for in sampling one I found it correspond exactly with the jesting descriptions which every elder Deddingtonian, including Miss Fowler, delights to give.

"They say you could tie a label to one and send it through the post a hundred miles—so hard it was."

"Deddington folk were supposed to save up all the scrapings from the candle drippings in the lanterns and put them in the pudding pies." This was also repeated to me by another baker, Mr. W. Course.

Miss Ruth Fowler, herself, quotes a story that gives a quaint, medieval flavour to their peculiar character—a King was journeying from Woodstock to Banbury through Deddington. At Woodstock they gave him gloves and at Banbury light cakes, but in Deddington something between the two, like leather but to be eaten.

Actually they contain a sort of glorified bread pudding in a very hard case. Miss Fowler told me that the outer crust has suet as an ingredient, this is filled with boiled plum pudding, the whole being afterwards baked. Once all the bakers here made them and they were sold at the Stalls. Boiled and baked like Simnel cakes, but with what a different result!

The Watchman had no sooner cried "four o'clock in the morning" than the town band started off to parade all round. It must have paused here and there to play like the Waits, for Mr. Tom Deeley, many years a carrier, whose memory goes back to the eighteen sixties, remembers music under his parents' windows at 5 a.m. and the wild feelings of excited, joyous anticipation it aroused. In the afternoon the band perambulated the town once more.

Leggings and winter clothing were purchased as a matter of course at this late November fair, and the stalls stretched from what was formerly Chisletts' Corner—now known as Smith's Corner; that is, along the Market Place to the house called the Hermitage. The stalls and booths had to keep strictly to that side for the middle of the square was full of pigs. Sheep thronged the portion of the market place which still bears the name of the Bull Ring, and they extended right along our present "Victoria Terrace," called then Hoof Lane, to where the pound was at Earl's Farm. From opposite the King's Arms, stretching across the Oxford-Banbury highway to some distance up the Hempton Road, there were sometimes as many as from six to seven hundred horses. That has been "the Horse Fair" from time immemorial, and iron rings for tethering are affixed here and there in the stone walls, as well as, formerly, posts at intervals with holes through which to pass the rope which secured the halters. That address proper ends at the police station corner and drovers no longer need space beyond.

Horned cattle were displayed all down the High Street, and one marvels to think that human ears amid the uproar could have heard the town band when it went round again in the afternoon.

OLD MICHAELMAS FAIR.

The August the 10th Fair must have been of much less importance than that of Old Martinmass (22nd of November), and the day after old Michaelmas, for no recollection of it remains traceable. But Michaelmas-tide Fair (Old Style before the reformation of the calendar in 1752 which the populace averred stole from them eleven days !) was written in red letters in the memory of our oldest inhabitant. An ox was roasted whole near what used to be the pool in the Market Place, and the meat was sold in shilling or sixpenny platefuls.

"Very good it was," said old William Hirons. And he further related that as many as fourteen fat "be-asts" used to be slaughtered for this festival. Beef was not merely on sale at the butchers' shops and stalls, but much of it was reserved for a sort of commercial hospitality. At this season it was usual for customers to settle up bills, and entertainment in true old English style was the rule.

"Beef and bread with their beer for all who called at the six principal public housen," explained Mr. Hirons, who used the ancient plural for 'houses'. "Tables laid in front of the housen, all for good o' the house, as they say." From his chuckles it was evident that those were grand times.

On the Wednesday in Whitsun week he recalled another gala season (Whitsun Ales ?) with more great doings which included "four bands playing in Church."

In January other junketings took place when rents were paid. William Wing's "Supplement to Marshall's Notes on Deddington" (published 1879) states that "the ox-roasting and hiring fair is abolished, but the November fair for hospitality, leather gaiters and puddings pies is well kept up."

In Walpole's British Traveller we find in the list of fairs, 'Doddington, August 21st (horses and sows). November 22nd. (ditto and swine).'

Fig 1 – Bird's eye map of Deddington by Joseph Wilkins (from the east)

Fig 2—Stone effigy in the church

Fig 3 — East end of Church (Joseph Wilkins)

Fig 4 — West end of Church (Joseph Wilkins)

Fig 5.—Castle house when a farm

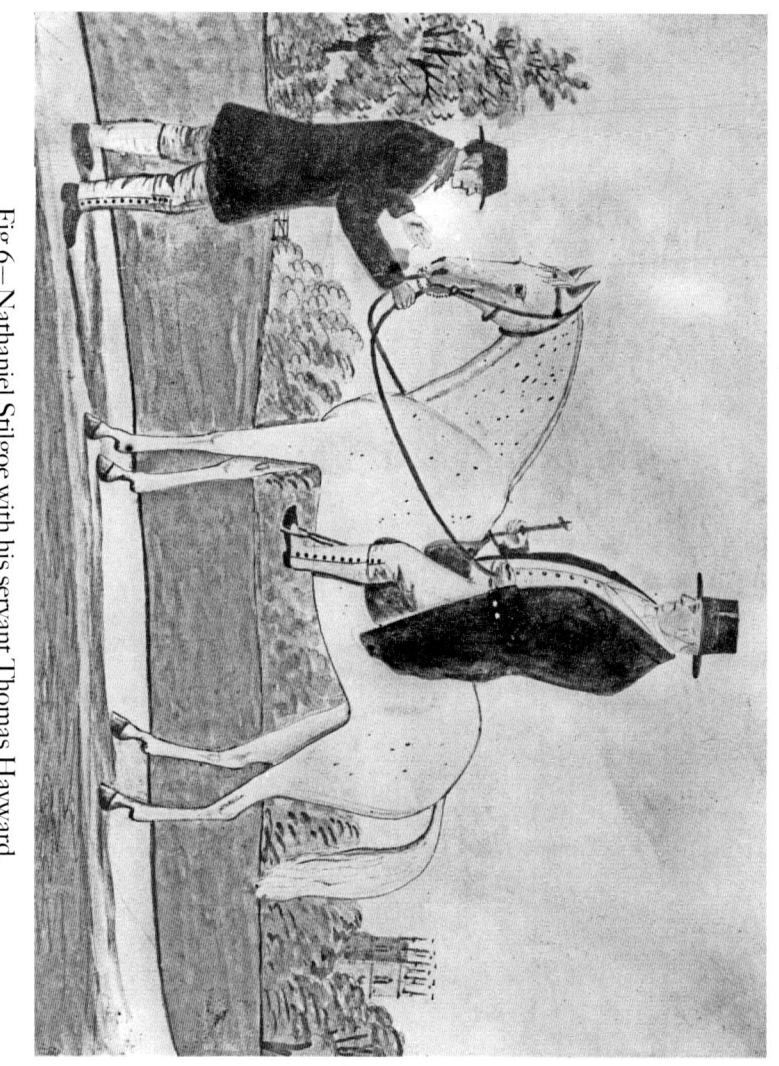

Fig 6—Nathaniel Stilgoe with his servant Thomas Hayward, from a sepia drawing by Joseph Wilkins

Fig 7 — The Pavillion (from a photograph)

Fig 8 — Portrait of John Knibbs, Town Crier and Ale Taster 'by appointment of Court Leet'

7. INNS AND COACHING DAYS.

'Long celebrated for the goodness of its malt liquor.'
(Oxfordshire Gazetteer for 1852).

'Six principal public houses' was the expression used by Deddington's oldest inhabitant describing the beef and beer hospitality customary when rent and bills were paid. These six would surely have been the King's Arms, Unicorn and Crown and Tuns, once coaching houses ; after them in importance, the Red Lion, Volunteer and Plough. The last is not now licensed, Mr. Eli Walker having turned it into a pork-butcher's and poulterer's shop. The old sign swings no more from its beautiful frame of wrought iron.

Besides these there were at least another probable nine or ten taverns and beer-houses in the town. The Three Horse Shoes, the Exhibition Inn, the Butcher's Arms ; the Ship in the Horse Fair (still marked by its stone mounting step) is well remembered. A Bear is rumoured as having been near by the Red Lion ; there was also a tavern on the site of Tucker's Stores, and two beer houses, one above and one below on Goose's Green, and another where stands Mr. B. Weaver's grocery store in Chapel Square. In addition the Quit Rents payable yearly, dated June 14th, 1710, mentions 'a messuage in New Street, formerly the Black Swan' and 'the house Thomas Makepeace lives in called the Bell', also in New Street.

It is queried whether the Bell was a former name for the old Plough in New Street as names were sometimes changed. Notably this was the case with the Volunteer which so lately as the last quarter of the 19th century was the Flying Horse. This has led to a surmise that the inn may in an older form have been the Flying Horse of John Elkington of 'Dedington' whose trading token, dated 1667, bore that device in its centre with 'His half peny' on the other side.

The Red Lion in the Market Square definitely links our present with the first part of the sixteenth century, prosaic as it now looks in its rough-cast new casing. Its association with the family of William Byllyng (whose altar tomb with mutilated brass inscription in the Lady Chapel of the Parish Church is described in an earlier chapter) is alluded to by the Rev. E. Marshall in his Notes :—

'There was formerly on the door of the Red Lion Inn a *ling* fish with a *bill* through the body, as the emblem of the family of Byllyng, (Rawl MSS., in the Bodleian Library).''

A ling, states the dictionary, is a fish resembling a cod, so called from its lengthened form (Anglo-Saxon 'lang' meaning 'long'). A bill would, of course, be familiar as a country implement, and the two combined were a good instance of picture writing. Its position on the Red Lion may, one supposes, have indicated either that the family lived there, or that a hostelry bore this good wool merchant's arms. No trace of any carving like the description exists, but the landlord, Mr. James Green, has lately found when digging, and has set up in the yard a really beautiful example of 17th century stone mason's skill. It is an oval stone with slightly curved surface, surmounted by the heads of Cherubim, the sides ornamented with ancanthus leaves at the upper edges. The interior thus framed is innocent of inscription or signs of one, suggesting that the whole may have been a mason and stone-cutter's advertisement of his art, or that unforeseen circumstances (the plague ?) may have stopped an order's completion.

Among the practically vanished taverns is the Three Horse Shoes which was opposite the Volunteer ; where it stood, Mr. John Compton, fishmonger and poulterer, has his shop and dwelling. The beer-houses on Gorse's Green have gone, and their foundations under more modern houses are all that remain of others. When Mr. Alexander Fortescue took down a derelict cottage facing Church Lane in order to improve his garden, the last vestige of the once Butcher's Arms was effaced.

The Exhibition Inn is inhabited by that necessary village official, the dustman and scavenger. But its fine deeply grooved stone arch doorway of the perpendicular (15th century) period at once arrests attention. This is obviously an addition belonging to a building far anterior. The demolition of some historic pile was doubtless taken advantage of and this fine architectural relic of many carried away piece-meal, incorporated. Probability points to the Pilgrims' Rest as the origin, the dismantling and razing of Deddington Castle being too remote from the date of the inn's other part. This hostelry may, itself, be reasonably classed with those vanished with yesteryear. But what a tragedy was that vanishing we may learn from Brewer's History, which written in 1813 says the destruction took place in 1811.

'There was pulled down,' he writes, 'about two years back, an extensive building of some interest which Gough mentions as 'an old inn, chiefly of stone, for pilgrims.' A neighbouring gentleman who examined this ancient structure immediately previous to its demolition, informs us that it then consisted of a north and south side, which bore marks of having been connected with each other at both ends by other buildings, so as to form a spacious court or quadrangle. The entrance was by a stone porch, through a large door which had a smaller aperture for common use. The small door had been decorated by heraldic devices, carved on the wood ; all of which were much defaced. On each side of the entrance were large apartments, separated by a stone wall of great thickness, in which were constructed the chimneys, and two flights of stone stairs, much worn away. The staircase on the left of the entrance led to the upper rooms on the right ; and the other on the right of the entrance led to the upper rooms on the left. All these apartments were wainscotted with oak, in carved and fluted panels ; and such of the ceilings as remained were ornamented with fret-work.'

Mr. Manchip in his Notes quotes a tradition that Piers Gaveston was imprisoned here and not in the Castle, but he remarks that the tradition is 'vague.'

The site of the Pilgrims' Rest is believed to be on the Banbury Road, on the same side as the School, but nearer to Deddington after crossing what is usually called Back Lane. The portion assigned to it by most authorities is in the garden extension belonging to the Hermitage, between the bordering lane and the Horse Fair, where indeed the holy man who gave his name to the property is supposed to have had his habitat.

The Plough is in yet another category ; for its massive, but not exceptional, elevation of gold coloured Cotswold stone, which the general form and 'drip courses' above the windows proclaim to be of the Jacobean domestic style not uncommon here—has a treasure and a mystery in the crypt beneath it. Mr. Marshall's Notes dismiss it in a few words :—'at the Plough Inn, in New Street, there is a cellar with a groined roof.' The History and Gazetteer of the County of Oxford, 1852, describes it as 'a vault used as a cellar, having groined arches supported by light columns, carved in freestone......of great antiquity and equal beauty.'

Brewer, the historian, notes it as 'the cellar of a dwelling now used as a public house, vaulted with groined arches of stone, springing at a short distance from the ground.' Mr. Manchip adds to his designation of 'a groined roof' the remark that there is 'the appearance of a walled-up passage.' Vaulting and supports seem to belong to the 'decorated' period of architecture (14th century).

The crypt may have been the chapel of a religious order, to which supposition the occurrence of the name 'Black ffryers' (Dominican monks so called from the black cloak worn over their white habit) in ancient records of the town gives colour. And this chapel may well have become from its secluded position one of the 'Houses of Prayer' where Mass was said in secrecy after reformation law made the 'old' religious observances a penal offence.

The 'walled-up' legend has given rise to numerous fables. The Castle and the Church have both been named as objectives. But, as Mr. Thomas Smith reasonably points out, the lie of the land would make subterraneous communication with either impracticable. Although it may have, before bricking up, led 'somewhere,' the prosaic explanation is that 'the other side'—if there was one—ended in some bakehouse or store-room no longer needed.

COACHING DAYS.

To consider our licensed inns is to halt, fascinated, before those which were coaching houses too. The King's Arms, standing in the Horse Fair and visible from the high road, is a gracious gabled hostelry, long and rather low, coloured creamy white. Petrol pumps stand where ostlers and stable lads once clustered and the stable yard has cars instead of carriages 'on the wash.' In Kelly's Directory for 1852 it figures both as Commercial and Posting House and was kept by a Miss Ann East. The 'Rival' and the 'Regulator' were the coaches calling at the King's Arms. The 'Rival' left for Oxford every morning at half-past eight, also every evening at a quarter before five for Banbury. The 'Regulator' went to Banbury, Leamington and Warwick every morning at 10.30, and every day to Oxford at 3.30 p.m., the Oxford coaches meeting the Great Western Railway trains for London.

In spite of modernity and mechanising of traffic, an atmosphere of the olden jollity and leisure lingers about bars and the parlour where Mr. R. S. Hall, 'mine host', told me the following story which seemed to bring young 'bloods', striped 'tigers,' postillions and post-horses right on to the threshold.

"A brave breakfast such as earned for Tom Brown, on his way to Rugby School, the stage coachman's praise was in those days considered an indispensable foundation for a journey. One passenger evidently thought so and meant to do more leisurely justice to the King's Arms bill of fare than the time-table allowed. With the cracking of the whip, a clatter of hooves and gay sound of the horn the 'Rival' was off !

What is a seat booked and paid for to another wedge of game pie ? But the young man was not so simple. "Hi there ! Stop thief ! he's away on the coach with your silver spoons ! After him quick !"

Host, chambermaids, ostlers troop in at the guest's alarm. Yes, a glance shows that a clearance of table silver has been made. Saddle a good horse and overtake the the coach—bring back the thief to justice !

Again the 'Rival' is at the door, the guest climbs nimbly into his vacant seat, but not before he has waved a careless hand towards the great plated coffee pot. "Look in there—you'll find your spoons inside, and thanks for plenty of time for breakfast."

The roll of Quit Rents, dated June 14th, 1710, gives an altered title—'Queen's Arms' to the same house, a pretty compliment to Queen Anne.

....

The Unicorn Commercial Inn is square and imposing with a beautiful unicorn in white and gold. It commands the Market Place. The 'Queen' left there every morning for Oxford at half-past ten, calling at the Crown and Tuns, the 'Queen' again calling at both houses every evening at a quarter to seven on its way to Banbury. The 'quality', as noted in the chapter dealing with the Pavilion, used the dressing-rooms here and at the King's Arms when making their toilets in preparation for a ball after archery or other day-time diversions. A similar connexion with the 'rest and refreshment' of members of the hunt, still exists, though to a lesser extent. A stirrup cup, or its modern equivalent, and a cigarette, is enjoyed within those wide old-world precincts, whose mirrors often reflect the tittivation of fair faces and hats and veils.

What must have been frequently first and last as a pull-up for travellers nearing or leaving Deddington for Oxford was the Fox and Crown at North Aston turn. Though a farmhouse it is still called the Fox, and looks what it was. The last licensee was a spinster lady, and the Fox as a house of entertainment may be said to have expired in an odour of sanctity. At ten o'clock precisely the bar closed, customers as they filed out bidding their hostess a respectful goodnight. Then did barman, barmaids and any other servants repair to the parlour for prayers, and so to bed, admirably contradicting the reputation of Deddington proper as set forth in its local rhyme.

8. SPORTS AND PASTIMES.

Dr. Plot, whose 'Natural Curiosities of Oxfordshire' were published first in 1676, alluding to riding at the Quintain, a sport which survived in Deddington after it had died out elsewhere, writes :—

"They first set a post perpendicularly in the ground, and then place a slender piece of timber on the top of it, on a spindle, with a board nailed to one end, and a bag of sand hanging at the other : against this board they anciently rod with spears ; now, as I saw it at Deddington in this county, only with strong staves, which violently bring abot the bag of sand, if they make not good speed away, it strikes them in the neck or shoulders, and sometimes perhaps knocks them from their horses ; the great design of the sport being to try the agility both of horse and man, and to break the board......"—further observing "this is now only in request at marriages, and set up in the way for young men to ride at as they carry home the bride, he that breaks the board being counted the best man."

This tilting was centuries earlier an exercise for military prowess ; it doubtless took place in our market square, surviving as part of the rough play that old rustic wedding parties expected. Dr. Plot stated furthermore that 'he found the sport in no part of the country but where Roman ways did run, or where some Roman garrison had been placed.' With regard to this last, Akeman Street, the Roman road from St. Albans to Bath, crossed our highway by Sturdy's Castle ; the famous Port-way also was in the vicinity of Aynho.

The evolution of the chase from necessary food hunting to a recreation needs no comment. It suffices here to state that the Heythrop meets several times during the season in the Market Place which presents an animated scene, especially of recent years when horse-boxes and cars assemble to save steeds and riders from the fatigue of the over-long journeys which a reduced number of packs causes. Meets are fewer, consequently they are more numerously attended. Foxes are strictly preserved and farmers wholeheartedly in favour of only 'sporting' methods being used against the enemy, whose short, sharp bark is occasionally heard at night in the village, followed by the discovery of ravaged poultry-yards. The hunt very fairly allows compensation for fowls thus killed.

Outdoor games do not seem to have been organized till lately. Our (recently deceased) centenarian, William Hirons, recalled "filling a sack with hay which we kicked all across the Market

Place." Now an adult Deddington football team plays in the Castle Grounds, also boys' Clubs belonging to the Church and Chapel have their football in a field lent by Mr. J. Bletsoe, horse-breeder and farmer.

When Mr. Wing was writing Deddington possessed a rifle corps with shooting range and butts, but he laments that the "once pleasant gatherings called Flower Shows have passed away." Fortunately these last were revived and this year's Show (1932) is nineteenth of the new series.

Seasonal games are of the usual kind. This year extra dryness brought tops in early, and in March bows and arrows (home-made) had a brief but enthusiastic reign ; but traffic has conquered the hoop. With warmer days pavements can be seen chalked for hop-scotch, and skipping ropes also come out in the Market Square.

MUMMERS.

Four years ago, on Boxing Day, the mummers were still going round the village. Those I saw were most of them from Clifton. They collected for local charities and sang, played concertinas and danced. Their songs had nothing more antique than the half-a-century old "My Grandfather's Clock," and their steps were mostly 'double shuffle,' but their get-up had traditional touches lingering. For example, there were old top-hats be-ribboned, and their flannel trousers adorned and tied with ribbons suggested the Morris. Also there was the time-honoured character with blackened face and one dressed up as a comic female.

Black-face linked these modern mummers with the memories of Mr. Hirons. This, he said, was Beelzebub ; pretty good evidence that in former days Deddington used to get the famous mumming legend of St. George and the Dragon played with its "here come I, Beelzebub." Our oldest inhabitant was here, however, so overwhelmed by the comical recollections of his boyhood that not a great deal could be gleaned between his chuckles. The mummers were, he said, all in rags and they brought a besom. Their address began :—

"A-room, a-room,
Here I come with my broom......"

They proceeded to introduce the members of the cast.

"Big head and little wit" and "here I come with my face a-fire," "I as ain't been yet," were all mentioned.*

Of the dancing that must have been popular in such a dancing county, no special memories seem to be cherished except that a few years back one Fiddler Smith died in St. Thomas' Street. And of another old man named Joseph Wood it is recorded, by many who still remember him, that he played the pipes and tabor.

A less happy sporting (?) memory of one Knibbs is that he fought a sheep dog for a wager and won.

Folk dancing, however, has been effectively revived and the local branch of the Women's Institute (founded in 1925) won in 1929 the Shield of the Oxfordshire Federation.

At our Women's Institute Socials two singing games are sometimes spontaneously played ; one of them, I believe, is in no printed collection. This is sung to the tune of 'A-hunting we will go !" The players arrange themselves as in 'Oranges and Lemons' and at the last line are caught prisoners in the same manner. It runs :—

"Oh a-hunting we will go,
A-hunting we will go ;
We'll catch a little fox
And put him in a box,
And never, never let him go !"

The other is published and well known. It is danced with linked hands in a circle, turning first one way and then reversing as they sing :—

"Sally go round the sun,
Sally go round the moon,
Sally go round the chimney-pots
On a sunny afternoon."

May Day this year was kept on Monday, the second of the month, and many children brought prettily arranged wild and garden flowers to the door. An improvement on the usual "To-day, to-day is the first of May ; please to remember the garland" was the song of a litle boy who came alone. The commencement has quite the olden touch.

"My gentlemen and ladies,
I wish you happy May,
I've come to show my garland
Because it is May Day."

* These terms and names of characters link our mumming tradition with the Buckinghamshire ; but an old inhabitant, Mr. John Gibbs, added particulars of 'Old Mother Wallopsee' with her black face. She has been included in the Version now played by the newly formed 'Deddington Morris Dancers and Mummers.' (May 1933).

THE PAVILION.

Where the historian Leland states so laconically 'there hath been a castle'—still remain the Castle Grounds. Here from about the middle of the nineteenth century till the first decade of the twentieth, situated on the right-hand side of the present bowling-green, stood the remarkable structure called the Pavilion. It was so large that it contained a spacious ballroom with musicians' gallery, cloakrooms and a refreshment room. The whole was covered by an immense roof of thatch.

Inside the ballroom walls were hung with glistening chintz in a floral design and at intervals gas jets were arranged round in star-like clusters. Dance music was provided by a band from Oxford, invariably including a harp.

The Society gatherings there were brilliant and exclusively 'County'. Deddington could have no share in those functions except such satisfaction as might be obtained from gazing upon the smart equipages which went towards the entrance gate full, returning empty to park in the market place. Sometimes the ball had been preceded by an Archery tournament, then it was the custom of ladies, whose homes were at a distance, to dress at the King's Arms or the Unicorn. Another chance for Deddingtonians to catch a glimpse of beauty, though in all probability voluminously cloaked.

The Castle Grounds Lodge, which is still inhabited as a dwelling, was in the hey-day of pavilion glory, the abode of George Jones, professional cricketer and groundsman, who was in charge of the Gentlemen's Cricket Club and the Archery, which were the outdoor attractions. From the Lodge to the pavilion site there is now only a rough track. Then it was a drive fit for the barouches, broughams and family coaches which drew up in succession at the doors, and passing on, sometimes assembled to the number of one hundred in the market place.

Mr. Robert Tucker, our postmaster for many years, relates that as a boy he remembers as many as four four-in-hand coaches there. Through the friendliness of a coachman well known to him, Mr. Tucker was, moreover, smuggled into that 'select' paradise— a most difficult adventure, for even after penetrating within the enclosure, again hurdles fenced off possible invasion—and he saw there such a scene as now-a-days would certainly not be matched. Gas constellations, shining flowery wall-hangings, and lovely ladies swaying and gyrating in billowy silks and tarlatans all frills and furbelows, graceful as bell-shaped flowers.

In the end the vogue for pavilion gaities waned, and finally, principally on account of the expense of keeping in repair its immense expanse of thatch, demolition was decided upon. A Banbury auctioneer put the effects to the hammer, but the profits did not cover expenses. A little of its concrete foundation still remains. Some years ago Mr. Robert Tucker attended a sale at the house of the late Mr. H. Cotton Risley. Among a lot of waste paper he found there the minute-book of the Pavilion Club, kept by Mr. Stratton of Croughton whose family had been among its chief supporters. It was a facetious chronicle with records of such fines as 'drinks all round' or 'penalty to be paid a bottle of port.'

An annual Flower Show, a bowling green and winter matches of the Deddington football Club is the extent of the recreation uses to which the Castle grounds are put. There is no cricket played there, nor any provision made for children's games—the children instead risking their lives (and other people's !) in the public thoroughfares. Cattle are occasionally turned into the Castle grounds, earning for the landlords a trifling sum.

Let us hope that when we have 'set our house in order' as regards drains and water supply—both being at present only 'good in parts'—the matter of a real village playground may be taken in hand.

So far Deddington has no cinema, relying on occasional dances, whist drives and concerts for entertainments. Formerly puppet shows were sometimes held at the (late) Exhibition Inn and companies of strolling players pitched their tents at the corner of 'Back Lane' by Deddington School. Their repertoire ranged from Shakespeare to 'Maria Marten, or the Murder in the Red Barn.' The Autumn of 1925 saw their last appearance. It was a 'washout' in both senses for they had ceased to draw and torrential rains drove them from under canvas into lodgings.

N.B.—The Flower Show Committee at a Meeting on the 25th November, 1932, decided that owing to lack of funds this must temporarily cease.

9. MILESTONES.

Population in 1801, 1,552. In 1829, 1,847. In 1831, 2,078. In 1841, 2,025. Last census (1931), 1,234.

Looking back from our present vantage ground certain outstanding events catch the eye, more prominent in a general survey than in chapters wherein local history is studied piecemeal.

With Mr. T. A. Manchip as guide it is interesting to pause in order to learn something about the battle of Deddington, 1643. He begins by quoting from Beesley's Banbury.

'In 1643, Lord Wilmot, in August, was appointed to the command of a strong body of the King's horse, which was stationed about Banbury to watch and if possible prevent the advance of the Parliamentarian forces to the relief of Gloucester. On the 20th the king in person took the conduct of the siege of the city.'

(May's Hist. Parl.)—'The Parliament ordered the Earl of Essex to relieve it, and on the 26th he began his march to Beaconsfield and afterwards proceeded to Brackley Heath, where the Earl awaited a reinforcement from London of the trainbands and other auxiliaries. These arriving on the 1st September his army amounted to 15,000 men. Essex took up his quarters at Aynho and sent a regiment forward that night to Deddington, under the command of Col. Middleton, who hearing of two regiments of the King's horse being there, first sent two companies of dragoons and a party of horse to approach the town. The King's horse thereupon retreated to a passage towards Oxford where Lord Wilmot was with 50 troops.

The next morning two Parliamentarian regiments, conducted by Col. Middleton and Sir James Ramsay, advanced to that pass where the King's army stood, in two great bodies; and after some skirmish gained the pass and placed dragoons to maintain it. The King's forces, however, drew up again towards it, and a very hot skirmish ensued, which lasted many hours. At length the King's troops made a retreat, but perceiving that Col. Middleton's marched back towards the main army, they sent a party of horse to fall upon his rear, who followed them through Deddington, but were beaten back through the town in some confusion.'

After the battle of Cropredy, June 29th, 1644, on that night and the next, (Sunday) the King slept at Williamscot, and on Monday, July 1st, set out with much military pomp, 'drum beating, colours flying and trumpets sounding' (see extract from Captain Symonds' Diary in Chapter 3 (Streets and Houses) through Aynho-on-the-Hill to Deddington, where that night the Army rested, the king sleeping at the Parsonage House. An exchange of prisoners with the opposing force seems to have been the principal event of that day, but Deddington was frequently after on the fringe of encounters, and constantly had troops quartered in the town.

War has left its trace in the name of 'Battle Thorn Hills'. Though this may refer to earlier fighting it probably dates from the Civil War, where on July 1st, 1644, the Royalist troops left Aynho to move along under the shelter of these hills whose northern face is thus called. In this way they would avoid the open road, following the contour by the Pest House (where a sword has been found ; also bullets and human bones in the arable field nearby, below the barn, known as Deddington Field Barn, belonging to Mr. Hugh W. Stilgoe). And in all likelihood they would have stopped to drink at the spring above the Pest House, called the King's Spring to this day.

Five years later, the 'Levellers' (as mentioned already) called the 'Green Men' from the sea-green colours they hoisted, quartered themselves at their 'Randescvous' (Deddington) from whence they issued a 'Declaration on behalf of the Oppressed People of the Nation.' The movement was crushed by Cromwell who had several of their leaders executed.

THE VOLUNTEER MOVEMENT IN DEDDINGTON.

Jackson's Oxford Journal for October 14th, 1865, publishes the orders for the 6th Oxon Rifles Deddington Corps for the week commencing Oct. 13th.

Company Drill in Market Place 5 p.m. Tuesday. by order of Henry Churchill, Ensign. And this :—*The Annual Inspection of the Sixt Oxon Rifles.* Deddington Rifle Corps assembled in the Market Place at 11 a.m., mustering between 40 and 50, and marched thence to the Castle Grounds. They were put through their exercises and complimented by the Inspecting Officer. 'After the inspection the members present were invited by Ensign Churchill to partake of an excellent cold collation, which he had kindly and considerately caused to be prepared under the Pavilion, an invitation which was gladly and promptly responded to.'

With regard to this there is a local joke, or rather jocular tradition, preserved in the birdseye view map of Deddington, photographed from the one in possession of Dr. G. H. Jones. Unfortunately this had to be on a much reduced scale. Taking a magnifying glass the detachment of volunteers can be seen drawn up by the town hall, while away far off in St. Thomas' Street is their drummer, beating the big drum, quite alone.

This map was made by Joseph Wilkins, a local self-taught artist who lived in the Style ; several of his drawings are reproduced in this 'Village History'. The goodness of the collation is supposed to be responsible for the drummer's absence of mind—and body. As this individual was John Knibbs, town crier, and 'Ale taster by appointment of Court Leet,' it was certainly a tribute to the excellence of Deddington's malt liquor. His photograph shows him to have been of a fine country type. John Knibbs died at the age of 94.

LIGHTING DEDDINGTON.

A company was formed in July 1862, called the Deddington Gas, Coke and Coal Company Limited, and on January the 7th, 1863, the following prospectus was issued :—The directors desire to remind their fellow townsmen that the introduction of gaslight into Deddington offers the tradespeople an advantage for carrying on their respective business, and would induce a large influx of persons to the town who now frequent other places for the purchase of their merchandise......' The legal firm of Messrs. Kinch & Co. were requested to make enquiries respecting a site where gasworks sufficient to provide 300 lights could be erected. The neat red brick house at the commencement of the Clifton road still called 'the Gas House' commemorates this first effort by its name. Gas was later supplied by the United District Gas Co., Adderbury. For the past year electric light has also been available through the Wessex Electricity Company, who have installed it in some of the shops and many dwelling houses, though road lamps are still lit by gas.

THE GREAT WAR.

Between pre-war and post-war lies so immeasurable a division it seems absurd to count its years as only four. Economic upheaval has followed in the wake of its terror, but material anxieties must never dim for us what were its glories—the spirit of honour and chivalry that answered the call of 1914, the dogged duty that carried on.

On the outbreak of war Deddington had a creditable number of Territorials, both in the Oxfordshire Hussars (Yeomanry) and the Oxfordshire and Buckinghamshire 1/4 Battalion of Light Infantry. These were, of course, mobilised on declaration of war and intensive training began. The first detachment of the Oxfordshire Hussars landed in France on September the 18th, 1914—three days only after the London Scottish, who were actually the first territorial regiment to disembark. Our county Yeomanry received their 'baptism of fire' at Messines, on October the 31st, 1914, in the first battle of Ypres. Subsequently the Oxfordshire Hussars took part in some of the fiercest fighting on the Western Front. Loos, Arras, the Somme, Vermelles, Amiens, Cambrai, the Sambre, St. Quentin, Gillemont Farm and Rifle Wood are among the engagements in which they fought, the four last-named being the scenes of their heaviest casualties. They were also among the first to suffer from poison gas attack on May 2nd, 1915.

Deddington Territorials of the Oxford and Bucks Light Infantry had to bide their time, chafing at the delay, till March the 30th, 1915, before landing in France. They had been training in Essex and were detained in the Eastern Counties till the invasion scare was over. Once on the Western Front they had not long to wait before getting under fire in the trenches of Ploegsteert Wood, ("Plug Street"), during the first week of April, 1915. Ypres, the Somme, Vimy Ridge, Festubert, Pozieres, are among the battles in French and Flemish Flanders on the list of this battalion. In December, 1917, they were sent into Italy to assist Italian troops against the Austrian offensive on the Piave. Here they were under a terrible bombardment on June 16th, receiving severe casualties.

The Oxfordshire and Buckinghamshire Light Infantry were dispersed in March, 1919, after exactly four years service overseas.

Among Deddington men who took part in the war were some attached to the regular army ; either on active service or in reserve. These were, of course, not necessarily in local units. As their records show, some fought—and died—in far distant areas of hostility. A few members of our Territorials were drafted into regiments for service in African and Asian theatres of war.

Dr. G. H. Jones and his partner Dr. G. M. Hodges both served in the Royal Army Medical Corps. Dr. Hodges was in France from 1914 to 1916. On his return Dr. Jones joined for active service, 1916 to 1918, being part of that time on hospital ships and part in Egypt. Dr. W. Turner, who held Sergeant's rank in the Volunteers, remained for medical duty in the place.

Unhappily, Deddington's War Memorial is, neither in its design nor its position—a remote part of the cemetery—worthy of **its glorious purpose.**

But, standing before it, criticism is silenced, for it is indeed 'Sacred to the memory of the men who fell in the Great War, 1914-1918.' These words are in the front. Below, and on either side are these names.

A. ADEY.   J. AUSTIN.   E. BLISS.   W. F. BOLTON.
R. P. BULL.   C. CALLOW.   W. J. CARVILL.
A. CASTLE.   J. H. CHECKLEY.   H. G. S. CHURCHILL
A. J. CHISLETT.   N. CHISLETT.   G. I. DAVIS.
S. H. DEELEY.   O. A. J. DORE.   W. J. DUNN.
A. J. ELL.   H. FREEMAN.   W. L. FRENCH.
W. A. GARDNER.   J. GODFREY.   A. GOMM.
H. GRACE.   H. GRIFFIN.   W. D. HANCOX.
W. R. HANCOX.   A. E. HANCOX.   F. HAWKINS.
J. F. HAWKINS.   B. HAWKINS.   J. W. HIORNS.
A. W. HUTT.   F. HUTT.   T. A. MANCHIP.
J. E. MUNDY.   P. PINFOLD.   A. SPENCER.
G. SYKES, Junr.   F. T. TUSTAIN.   M. J. TUSTAIN.
J. E. TWISSELL.   W. A. WEAVER.   B. WHEELER.
G. H. WHITE.   W. WILKINS.   A. E. YERBURY.

At the back of the memorial is inscribed : "Live thou for England, we for England died."

A brass memorial tablet in the church again commemorates the names of those who made the Supreme Sacrifice ; nearby are several wooden crosses, among them those from the graves of the three brothers Hancox, and of 2nd Lieutenant Ronald Page Bull, killed a few days before Armistice, aged 19.

Above the brass tablet hangs the wreath of laurels and Haig poppies placed there annually at the Armistice Service by the Deddington branch of the British Legion, which forms a centre of comradeship and aid for local ex-service men.

Deddington never came under enemy fire, the nearest aerial bombardment being over Derby. But Deddington saw the Germans as prisoners working on local farms. These were for the most part poor country lads, drawn into the universal whirlpool, grateful for the peacefulness of their surroundings and the humanity of their employers.

At the time of writing, work is scarce and agriculture depressed. But in spite of all this there is a glorious note of hopefulness sounded in each succeeding report on the condition of the children. The medical inspection of schools has wrought wonders. This and the appointment of official women health visitors have definitely raised the physical standard of the rising generation, and thereby the mothers have been stimulated and helped. In Deddington an Infant Welfare Society meets monthly under the supervision of a medical man with the health visitor in attendance, who give useful advice and information, and help where further treatment is required.

The Women's Institute, affiliated to the Oxfordshire Federation of Women's Institutes, founded here in the autumn of 1925 with a membership of over 70, still carries on with vigour, numbers being often above, but seldom below, the first enrolment. Its object ('for Home and Country') is kept well uppermost, and the remark made when it was started, that it was the first social meeting place for all women ever known in Deddington, still holds good, and has immensely increased our understanding of one another.

APPENDIX. I.

(From the Rev. E. Marshall's Deddington). List of Rectors, or other Early Clergy.

Ranulph Brito (Le Bret) Rector, died 1247.
Ethelmar de Valence was instituted 1247.
John Walrond was instituted 1269.
Nicholas de Marnham, Rector, died 1292.
William de Holecote was instituted 1292.
Adam de Bernentone was Vicar (qu. substitute of the Rector) 1312.
Robert de Harwedon resigned 1318.
William Aylmer, instituted 1318, died 1328.
William de Neuport, instituted 1328, died 1332.
Remigius was Chaplain of Deddington circ. 1332.
John de Goldyngham was instituted 1332.
Hugh de Neuton, Rector, died 1345.
William de Annem was instituted 1345.

The interval between 1345 and 1523, during which no name is mentioned, follows the cessation of the institution of Rectors, on the appropriation of the Church by the Dean and Canons of Windsor.

VICARS AND OTHERS.

William Farmer was Vicar in 1523.
Thomas Hotchynson was Vicar in 1534.
Thomas Hodgkinson (qu. the same as the preceding) was Vicar in 1534-43.
John Brown was instituted in 1543, resigned 1558.
John Gryffth was described by testators as "my ghostly father," (qu. Chantry priest) 1545.
William Edlynson was instituted 1558.
Christopher Allsop was instituted 1565.
William Bennett was instituted 1595, died 1619.
John Edmunds, B.A., was instituted 1619, died 1630.
William Bradenell, M.A., was instituted 1630, died 1654.
William Hall, Vicar in 1644, died 1654.
James Wyer, Vicar in 1660 died 1664.
Samuel Northcote, M.A., was instituted 1664.
Clifton Stone was Minister (Par. Reg.) qu. Vicar, 1667.
Jaspar Cann was Minister (Par. Reg.) qu. Vicar, in 1669, 1670.
Jeremiah Wheate, Vicar in 1673, died 1697.
Charles King, instituted 1697, died 1700.

Richard Short, instituted 1700, died 1747.
John Short, B.A., instituted 1747, died 1752.
John Henchman, M.A., instituted 1752, died 1790.
John Faulkner, B.A., instituted 1790, died 1802.
Richard Greaves, instituted 1802, resigned 1836.
William Cotton Risley, M.A., instituted 1836, resigned 1848.
James Brogden, M.A., instituted 1848, died 1864.
James Turner, B.A., instituted 1864, resigned 1877.
Thomas Boniface, M.A., instituted 1878, resigned 1924.
Maurice Frost, M.A., instituted 1924.

For 1802 as the date of John Faulkner's death and Richard Greaves' institution, William Wing in his 'Supplement' substitutes 1822, calling it 'an erroneous date twice repeated.' He writes 'it was in 1822, not 1802, that Vicar Faulkner died and was succeeded by the Rev. Richard Greaves ; the present writer (William Wing) born in 1810, well recollects the Rev. John Faulkner in the reading desk facing north with a clerk's seat below him and a pulpit above.' The list in the church gives 1821 and 1822 as death and institution dates respectively.

The Latin Rolls of the Court of the Prior of Bicester supply one name that helps to fill the interval mentioned between 1345 and 1523. The entry is as follows :—"Walter Cheyne, Vicar of Dadyngton is granted a toft (a messuage with right of common) hard by Sotty Lane." (Satin Lane, now often called St. Thomas' Street).

The latter is named, not after a Saint, but after one Thomas Parish who owned land there.

APPENDIX. II.

Measurements (taken from Mr. T. A. Manchip's Notes).
The Parish Church. The mark on the N.W. corner of the tower is 425 ft. above the level of the sea. (Mark 16in. above ground).
Dimensions of the Parish Church.

	ft.	in.
Length from inside west door to east end	158	10
Length of Nave	105	0
Length of Chancel	53	0
Width of Nave including Aisles	71	6
Width of Chancel	18	0
Width of Nave without Aisles	24	6
Width of South Aisle	22	0
Width of North Aisle	20	0

Weight of Bells.

	Cwts.	Qrs.	Lbs.	Note.
Treble.	7	0	8	C sharp
Second	7	1	25	B.
Third	9	0	16	A.
Fourth	10	1	27	G sharp
Fifth	12	3	7	F sharp
Tenor	17	0	10	E.

They were cast by Mears of Whitechapel, London, and the inscription on them is :—"Thos. Mears, late Lester, Pack and Chapman of London, fecit, 1791."

The small bell (ting-tang) is older, and bears the inscription :- "Antony Basely. Richard Large. C.W. 1649."

APPENDIX. III.

ARMORIAL GLASS IN DEDDINGTON CHURCH, A.D. 1574.

I. Gu a lion rampant Or.
II. Quarterly Gu. and Or in the first quarter a mullet (Vere).
III. Barry Arg and Az an orle of martlets Gu (De Valence).
IV. Quarterly 1 and 4 Gu a castle triple towered Or (Castile)
V. Or a fess Gu.
VI. Quarterly Ar and Gu in the 2nd and 3rd quarter a fret Or, over all a bend Sa. (Despenser).
VII. Barry nebulée Arg and Sa on a chief Gu. a lion passant Or.
VIII. A virgin couped at the breast crowned within a bordure nebulée.
IX. Or a lion rampant Sa.
X. Or a cross engrailed Sa.
XI. The Arms of Mortimer (Barry of six Or and Az. an inescutcheon Arg. on a chief of the first three grales between the gyronnies of the second).
XII. Gu a fess between six cross crosslets Or (Beauchamp).
XIII. Quarterly 1 and 4. Arg. a lion rampant crowned Gu 2 and 3 Quarterly Arg. and Gu. on each quarter a cross patée counterchanged of the field.
XIV. Quarterly 1 and 4 Barry of Six (untinctured) 2 and 3 Or. three boar's heads couped Sa.
XV. Gules, three bars dancette Or.
XVI. Gu a fess between eight bittels Or. 5 and 3 (Beauchamp).

XVII. Quarterly 1 and 4 Barry nebulée Or and Sa. (Blount) 2 and 3 Arg a lion rampant Gu.

XVIII. Az. a bend cotised between six Martletts Or. Over the Shields XVI, XVII and XVIII is written "John Beauchamp, Knight and Clounte, esq. and Allice thes wiffe/thes iij"
Knelyngin glass armor in glas wth the Cotes of Armes. John (Pope) et Margreata uxor ejus and gaverell* and Anne his children wch Margret died the last of August MCCCI. William Pope and Julian and Margret his wiffes wch W dessessed the XXVth of Marche Mdxxiii."
Askochen in Mr. byllings house (at Deddington).

I. Arg. a cinquefoil gu. on a chief of the last a demi-lion rampant Or. impaling, two coats per fess (!) Az. a fess engrailed between three woman's heads couped at the breast Or. (2) Erm, a lion rampant Az. crowned Or.
Copied from the Visitation of the County of Oxford A.D. 1574.

* Gabriel.

APPENDIX. IV.

TRANSLATION OF DEED RELATING TO DEDDINGTON.
(1607).

This is the Deed of Alice Stamper to all the faithful in Christ to whom the present Deed shall come, from Alice Stamper of Deddington in the County of Oxford, widow, eternal salvation in the Lord.

KNOW that I the aforesaid Alice of my sole widowhood and lawful power have surrendered given and by this present Deed confirmed for the sum of thirteen shillings and four pence sterling paid into the hands of me the aforesaid Alice to Richard Gylkys of the aforesaid Deddington husbandman the whole of that my cottage situate and lying in the new suburb of the aforesaid Deddington between the farm and messuage of the Dean of Windsor on the North and a certain enclosure of our Lord the King on the South with one small curtilage Barn and garden adjacent thereto with all other appurtenances; which cottage barn and garden came to me the aforesaid Alice by inheritance after the death of John Nycoll my father.

The aforesaid Richard Gylkys his heirs and assigns TO HAVE AND TO HOLD the aforesaid cottage with its curtilage barn and garden aforesaid with their appurtenances in perpetuity from the Chief Lord of the Fee by the services due and of right accustomed.

And I the aforesaid Alice and my heirs will guarantee, to the aforesaid Richard Gylkys his heirs and assigns, the whole of the aforesaid cottage with its curtilage barn garden and other appurtenances against all men, and will defend them in perpetuity by these present and in witness thereof I the aforesaid Alice have appended my seal to this my present Deed.

WITNESS : William Byllyng of the aforesaid Deddington, gentleman, Robert Gleyford, Henry Watson, Richard Stylgoe, and others. Given on the 11th day of November in the twenty-second reign of King Henry VIII (1532) in the presence of John Gys, John Coke and William Nurse, Bailiffs of the aforesaid Deddington and of the aforesaid Richard Gylkys for deliberation possession and seizure.

ENGROSSED and examined by Hugo Handley supervisor of our Lord King James of 1607.

TRANSLATION OF DEED RELATING TO DEDDINGTON.
(1443).

This is the Deed of John Scoler.

KNOW ALL MEN present and future that we John Scoler of Northampton and Katherine my wife, daughter and heir of William Ireland lately of Deddington in the County of Oxford give concede and by this our present Deed confirm to Richard Westley, hosier, of the aforesaid Deddington, the whole of this our messuage with its garden and appurtenances which formerly belonged to the aforesaid William Ireland and which we have in the aforesaid Deddington situated between the tenement of John Admond on the one side of the tenement of John Jenyn on the other side ;

The aforesaid Richard Westley his heirs and assigns TO HAVE AND TO HOLD the aforesaid messuage with its garden and appurtenances of the Chief Lords of the Fee by the services due and of right accustomed. And we the aforesaid John Scoler and Katherine my wife and our heirs will guarantee the aforesaid messuage with its garden and the appurtenances to the aforesaid Richard Westley, his heir and assigns against all men.

WITNESS THEREOF we have appended our seals to this our present Deed. Given at the aforesaid Deddington on the 12th day of December in the twenty-second year of the reign of Henry VI after the conquest.

WITNESSES : William Mylcheburn, Thomas Syr, William Herncastell, of the aforesaid Deddington and many others.

APPENDIX. V.

A Copy of the Deed
Inrolled from
Mr. Wickham to
Mr. John Lane &
his wife
1 May 1635
11 Car 1.
No 65.

This Indenture made the ffirst Day of May Anno Dni 1635 And in the Eleaventh yeare of the Raigne of our Sovaigne Lord Charles by the grace of God of England Scotland ffrance and Ireland Kinge Defender of the faith &c Betweene Thomas Wickham of ffifield in the County of Southton Esqe on thone pte And John Lane of Clifton in the pish of Daddington als Deddington in the County of Oxon gen and ffrances his wife on the other parte Witnesseth that the said Thomas Wickham for and in Consideracon of the Sume of Three hundred and fifty poundes to him before hand payd by the said John Lane and ffrances his wife and for other Valuable Consideracons Doth hereby grant bargayne and sell unto the said John Lane and ffrances his wife and the heires of the said John All that the Guild or ffraternity of the Holy Trinitie and St. Mary of Daddington als Deddington in the said County of Oxon lately dissolved And all Messuages landes tenemts Rentes services and hereditamts whatsoever in the parish of Daddington aforesaid to the said Guild or ffraternity belonginge or appteyneinge or heretofore had knowne lett used taken or reputed as pte pcell or member of the said late Guild or ffraternitie with all and singuler their apptenncs sometimes heretofore in the tenure or occupacon of Sr Anthony Cope Knight or his Assignes parcell of the Landes and possessions of the Dutchie of Lancaster And all and singular Messuages houses edifices shopps Sellers Sollers Courtes Curtelages Stables Dovehouses Gardens orchardes landes grounds Meadowes pastures woodes underwoodes furzes heathes Woodes Marishes backsides wayes wastes Comons orchardes landes pffitts comodityes emolumts and hereditamentes whatsoever with their apptennces of what nature or knde soever they be or by what name or names soever they were called or known situate lyinge and beinge within the pish of Daddington aforesaid to the said Guild or ffraternity Messuages Landes Tenemts hereditamts and pmisses or any pte or pcell thereof belonginge or in any wise appteyneinge or accepted reputed Deemed taken or knowne as pte pcell or membr thereof or of any pte or pcell thereof And all other the Messuages Lands Tenemts and hereditemts whatsoever of the said Thomas Wickham situate lyinge and beinge in the towne, fieldes, parish or precincts of Daddington aforesaid Except and allwayes reserved forth of these prtes one Messuage or tenemt & one yard land with their appurtennces in Daddington aforesaid now or late in the tenure or occupation of one Thomas Nutt or of his Assignes, and one other Messuage or tenemt and two yard lands with their apptennces in Daddington aforesaid now or late in the tenure or occupation of one Thomas Maynard or of his Assignes, and one other Messuage or tent and halfe yard landes with the apptennces in Daddington aforesd nor or late in the occupacon of Nicholas Rand or of his Assignes and one other Close with the apptennces now or late in the tenure or occupacon of Edward Maynard or of his Assignes in Daddington aforesaid To have and to hold the said Guild or ffraternitie Messuages lands tenemts hereditamts and premisses and evy pte & pcell thereof with their apptennces (except before excepted) unto the said John Lane and ffrances his wife and the heires of the said John Lane for ever In witnes whereof the said ptyes to these psent Indentures Interchangably have sett their handes and seales the Day and yeare frst above written :/:

Thomas Wickham

Sealed and Delived in
the psence of
Wm Seymor
Willm Mundy
Geo : Hearne
Cha : Thurman

Recognit coram me Johe Michell
Mil in Cancellar Magro 2do
Maii 1635
          Jo. Mychell

In dors Claus Cancellar
Infrascript Domini Regis Quarto
die Maii Anno Infrascripto
      p Martin Hardrett

Vera Copia exaiata Decimo quarto die
Aprilis 1652 p nos Ambre Holbech sen
   Sam Holbech Jun

APPENDIX. VI.

(From the Oxford Will Registry).
Will of Anthony Stilgoe de
Dadington in Co. Oxford. Husbandman.
Dated 28th May. 1606.

'In the name of God Amen.

I Anthonie Stilgoe of Dadington in the county of Oxon, husbandman, sicke in body but of perfect mind and memory (praise be God) doe make this my last Will and testament in manner and followinge. Fyrst I give and bequeathe my soule into the hand of

— 87 —

the Almighty God, trustinge to be saved by the onlie death and passion of my Lord and Saviour Jesus Christe, and my body to the earth from whence it was taken, my worldly goods thus I doe dispose.

Fyrst I give unto ye Mother Church iiijd. Then I give unto sonne Thomas Stilgoe my seaven horses and coltes, exceptynge the herriot. My plows, cartes and harrowes with plowe tymber, carte tymber and harrowe tymber, and all the furniture to them. Then I give unto him more all my part of the king's and Deanes land belonging unto me this year, conditionally that he shall discharge all and all manner of debts that I do now owe any man, and that he shall put in sufficient secureity for the discharge thereof unto my wyffe and her assignes.

Item. I will that the said Thomas Stilgoe shall well manure and till one yarde lande belonging unto my wyffe. Also one yard land of Theobaldes land during the time of her lyffe.

Item. I give unto her more my cropp of Hay that lyeth this year in Bugbrooke. And yerely during the tylledge of Theobaldes Land iiijs of lawfull English money for each year.

Item. I will that my said son shall upon a day's warninge bring home the said two yarde lands croppe to my house where now I dwell, and shall yerely fetch home to the said house two loads of wood during the natural lyffe of my said wyffe and shall yerely carry all such soil as shall be made unto the said two yard lands and likewise all kind of carriadges of stone and morter for building.

Item. I give unto Nicholas Lynnet iiij bushells of corne, ij of manstlin and ij of barlie and iiij sheepe and to each of his children a sheep a peece runninge.

Item. I give unto Nicholas Charman iiij bushells of corne, ij of manstlin and ij of barlie and iiij sheepe and to each of his children a sheepe a piece runninge.

Item. I give unto my godsons iiijd a peece.

Item. I give unto the poore at the day of my funerall to be disbursed Xs in money.

Item. I give unto my sister Elizabeth Stilgoe ijs VId in money. All the residue of my goods chattells and Household stuffe unbequeathed as well moveable and unmoveable I give and bequeathe unto my wyffe Elizabeth Stilgoe, whome I will to be the only executrix to this my last Will and testament. One Kymbell's house situate and being in Castell Street during her natural lyffe charging her to see my body honestly brought unto the earth and to see my funeral discharged. The overseers to this my last Will and testament I ordeine to be Thomas Gylk and Richard Tredwell to whome I give XXd and pleece to take pains to see this my last Will and testament to be executed and performed,

and to William Bennett ijs. In witness whereof I have putt my marke the day of yere above wrytten in the presence of Nicholas Linnett and Nicholas Charman and Thomas Stilgoe.
Anthonie Stilgoe. His mark.
Proved at Dadington Co. Oxford by
  Elizabeth Stilgoe on the 25th September,
1606. relict executrix.
  Consistory Court of Oxford.'

 This will is interesting not only as typical of a husbandman, or yeoman, of those times, but the various farming implements, measurements, method of writing numerals, etc. will all be noted as characteristic.

 Mr. H. E. Stilgoe, Anthonie's descendant, contributes the following information regarding localities mentioned.

 'Bugbrooke, sometimes referred to in Deddington documents as Bugbrook Butts, lies to the south of Harbour's Hill Road. This road is the narrow lane leading out of the main Banbury to Oxford road ; it runs from west to east and occupies the ridge just above Dr. Turner's house. Harbour's Hill is that portion of the land lying between Satin Lane and the little brook on the south side of Harbour's Hill Road. Satin Lane is now called St. Thomas' Street, I believe.'

 Mr. Stilgoe still owns a small field in Bugbrook Butts, which goes with the house in Council (formerly Castle) Street. Of this and the adjoining land the Stilgoe family have been Copy holders since the time of Anthony Stilgoe and probably before. It was part of the Windsor Manor until 1917 when Mr. H. E. Stilgoe enfranchised it.

 The numbers, or rather symbols of numbers, denoted by strokes are deciphered thus : ij is two ; iiij is four ; Xs is ten shillings in money ; ijs VId is two shillings and sixpence.

 The expression "yard land" used in the Will is a measure, the quantity thereof varied in different parts of the country. Mr. Stilgoe writes :—'I can throw some light upon this from a note made in 1640 by Zachary Stilgoe as follows :—

 "At a Court of Survey for Christ Church, Oxford, 16 October 1640.

 "How many acres do belong to a yard land ?

 "To some more, to some less, but we do guess there will be "about 18 acres in our common field measure, but not by "statute measure, at various places the yard land is determin-"ed by the number of beasts kept, i.e. at Deddington for each "yard land 2 horses, two beasts and thirty sheep."

APPENDIX. VII.

Extracts from the Diary of the Rev. William Cotton Risley (lent by Major Reginald Roberts, present owner of Deddington House, now known as Deddington Manor.

1836.
May 9th. Took possession of Deddington House.
Sept. 25th. Mr. Brayne sent for and another very fine boy born.
Sept. 30th. Mr. Wyatt the carver and gilder from Oxford came to see our Church and arrange about a painting for an altar piece—"Dead Christ and Three Marys" price 15 gns.
Oct. 1st. ......presented the Church and parish with a new Communion cloth this day.
Oct. 18th. Went to Oxford to take certain oaths as Vicar of Deddington and to qualify at the Sessions as Magistrate.
Oct. 22nd. Mr. Underwood, architect from Oxford, came to examine the Church and crypt and to give his opinion on the alterations I had made and to send me a plan for a new pulpit and reading desk.
Oct. 29th. Franklin's man began putting up the inner door of the Church yesterday by my order and at my expense—to be covered with drab cloth.
Oct. 31st. Franklin put up the looking glass in our drawing-room. Endeavoured to stop the bonfire in the middle of the Town, near the Town Hall and close Sir J. Calcotts' (?) house. A boy named John Gibbs was very impudent. I gave him a back-handed slap of the face.
Dec. 24th. Mr. Wyatt's son, carver and gilder from Oxford, came and put up in the Chancel an old painting "A Dead Christ with the Three Marys."
Dec. 26th. A very deep and drifting snow. No coaches able to reach the Town. The Van 12 hours coming from Oxford with 9 horses.

1837.
[Gaieties at Aynho Park recorded]..........
The coach to Oxford by which some guests intended to return being 1½ hours late and quite full, they had to post it to Oxford.
Feb. 27th. A case tried at the Assizes between Deddington and Clifton, the latter wanted to be a separate parish—they failed and refused to pay and collect rates.
Mar. 25th. Went to the Vicarage and examined the state of the Chesterton oak boards previous to putting up a new pulpit and reading desk in Deddington Church.

May 3rd. Went up to the Kings Arms in the evening and paid Lord Carrington's agent my rent......for a certain dwelling house and premises with pleasure ground, the same being mortgaged to Lord Carrington by S. Churchill, Esq., the late proprietor, now a Bankrupt.

May 24th. The Princess Alexandrina Victoria attained her majority this day—heir apparent of the English Throne. The bells rang at intervals during the day by my order.

June 6th. ......Mr. Graham, the Aeronaut, ascended from Oxford in a balloon at 4 p.m.

1839.
Feb. 7th. Attended a large meeting at Banbury for the purpose of petitioning against the repeal of the present corn laws.

Mar. 5th. Remained in Court the whole day from 8 a.m. up to 7 p.m. Heard the trial of Joseph Chapman, Gamekeeper to Lord Dillon, for the murder of James Cottonham by shooting him with his double-barrelled gun. He was found guilty and left for execution.........

Apr. 27th. Holford completed his 8th year.

June 27th. Sale of Deddington House. Went to Banbury...... to attend a sale of Mr. S. Churchill's property at Deddington and elsewhere, he being a bankrupt. I bought his late house and farm adjoining at the sum of £8,920 and the timbers to be valued. I bought Appletree farm at £2,720 and a piece of freehold ground adjoining at £105.

Oct. 8th. James Churchill agrees to sell his house and a strip of ground adjoining our present pleasure ground.

Nov. 15th. The stone planking and paving in front of the house from the kitchen entrance to the yard gates was finished today.

Nov. 19th. ......9 acres with a cottage adjoining our pleasure ground of Mr. John Calcutt for the sum of £1,800......

Dec. 6th. Moved Hoyle Hill gate down to a new situation in consequence of my having purchased the orchard and premises (late Whetton's).

1840.
Sept 15th. New Organ. Our new organ arrived in safely at about a quarter after 10 p.m., drawn by my teams and accompanied by Mr. Chambers, the builder and his man. The bells struck up a merry peal.......

1841.
Jan. 4th. I went up to Oxford with Mr. Loveday (of Williamscote) to attend the Sessions. We voted an address of congratulation to the Queen and Prince Albert on the birth of the Princess Royal of England.

Jan. 14th. Busy in the farmyard, giving directions for distribubution of 2 faggots to every family. Six waggon loads went out.

Major R. Roberts adds this note :—'Old Mr. Wm. Risley died and left the property to his eldest son Holford Risley who died unmarried. Let to Col. Murray durng short time. Colonel Murray bought it about 1895. Left it to his brother Mr. Charles Murray, who only survived a short time and left it to his wife, whose daughter was Mrs. Holford. Captain A. Holford and his daughter came here in 1921, after Mrs. Holford's death. Stayed 7 years and sold it to Colonel Beckwith Smith in 1928, who sold it to us.' (1932).

APPENDIX. VIII.

Some Field names, contributed by Mr. William Page, Farmer of Deddington.*

Fishers 107	Castle Side 187
Barson Hill 94	Dairy Ground 147
Windmill Field 208	Oak Tree Ground 146
Breach 451	Basil 222
School Ground 500	Picked Ground 223
King's Spring 439	Hill Ground 224
Pest House 440	Plank Meadow 143
Wand Brook 160	Eyford Hill 205
Kite Moor 132	Round Hill 393
Little Thistle Hill 425	The Butts 391
Thistle Hill 426	Chapman's Leys Closes 188
The Lake 423	Town's End 480
The Fishers 174	Long Ground 465
Malinger 135	Battle Thorn 388
Hoyle Hill 166	Tank Ground 358
Barn Ground 418	Wet Lands 381
Lower Breach Furlong 420 444	
Westmore Hill 446	

Mr. Page states that most of the other fields are called Dairy Ground, Barnfield or meadow.

* Numbers given are from the Ordnance Survey Map, Edition of 1923, Oxfordshire Sheet X13. Scale 208.33 feet to one inch.

APPENDIX. IX.

LIST OF BIRDS IN THE DISTRICT.

(Contributed by Miss H. Loveday, Deddington).

Resident.

Blackbird. Blackheaded Gull. Bullfinch. Chaffinch. Cornbunting. Crow. Dabchick. Goldfinch. Greenfinch. Gull. Heron. Hedge Sparrow. House Sparrow. Jackdaw. Kestrel. Kingfisher. Kittiwake (passing over). Lark. Linnet. Magpie. Missel Thursh. Moorhen. Nuthatch. Owl, (barn, brown and little). Partridge. Pheasant. Redpole. Redwing. Robin Redbreast. Sparrow. Sparrowhawk. Snipe. Starling. Stock dove. Teal. Thursh. Tit, (blue, cole, great, long-tailed and marsh). Tree creeper. Water wagtail (pied). Wild Duck. Woodpecker, (greater spotted, lesser spotted and green). Wren. Gold-crested Wren. Yellow Hammer.

Summer Visitors.

Blackcap. Chiff-chaff. Cuckoo. Flycatcher. Garden Warbler. Greater White-throat. Lesser White-throat. Hawfinch. House Martin. Nightingale. Sandpiper. Sedge Warbler. Shrike (red-backed). Swallow. Swift. Tree Pippet. Turtle dove. Wagtail (grey-backed). Wheatear. Willow Wren. Whinchat. Wood Wren. Wryneck.

Winter Visitors.

Fieldfares. Redshanks. Redwings. Wigeon. Woodcock.

N.B. This list is not contributed as exhaustive. Some of the resident birds enumerated are rare, and many of the visitors only occasional.

INDEX.

Adderbury. 42.
Akeman Street. 70.
Alfred, King. 12.
Anne, Queen. 69.
Apletree or Appletree fam.
    21, 25, 35, 38, 49, 53, 57.
Aynho. 31, 41.

Banbury. 14, 40, 63.
Basset. 10, 11, 56.
Becket. 20.
Belcher fam. 26, 52, 53.
Beresford, Ralph de. 18.
Bicester. 10, 56.
Bissell, H. 25, 34.
Blacklow Hill. 12.
Bohun. 8, 9.
Boniface, Rev. T. 27.
Brodrick, G. 26.
Brito, R. de. 17.
Bryant, the Misses. 34.
Burton, W. 50.
Bustard. 35, 58.
Bylling. 20, 56, 65.

Calcutt, J. 34.
Carriers. 45.
Cartwright. 41, 52.
Cary. 25, 35.
Castle. 10.
Charles I. 15, 28.
Charles II. 22.
Cherwell. 6.
Cheyne, W. 37.
Churchill fam. 34, 49, 76.
Clement, Pope. 9.
Clifton. 6, 42.
Cromwell. 22, 76.
Coggins, Lawyer. 49.
Cropredy. 15, 31.

Davies, H. J. 26.
Deddington. Battle of. 75.
    Civil War. 15, 31, 76.
    Court Rolls. 35.
    Fairs. 62.
    Local Rhymes. 40, 42.
    Manors. 8.
    Parliamentary Borough. 7.
    Gas Company. 77.
    War Memorial Names. 79.
    Various Spellings. 7.

Deeley, Thomas. 38, 63.
Directories (Trades). 44, 45.
Downe, Earl of. 47.
Dyve, Guy de. 10.

East, Ann. 44, 68.
Edmunds, J. 35, 58.
Edward, Confessor. 8.
    II. 12.
    III. 9.
    IV. 9.
    VI. 9, 50.
Elizabeth. (Princess at Hatfield). 46.
    Queen. 14.
Elkington, John. 53, 65.
Emberlin fam. 42.
Ethelfled. 12.

Falkland, Lord. 31.
Fardon, J. and T. 42.
Faulkner, Duffel. 12, 28, 49.
Faulkner, Rev. J. 54.
Field, Samuel. 49.
Fowler, Miss R. 62.
Franklin. 32, 39.
Frost, Rev. M. 24, 27.

Garner (Architect). 32.
Gaveston, Piers. 10, 67.
Great War. 77.
Greaves, Rev. R. 27, 54.
Griffin, W. 52.
Griggs, F. L. 29.

Hall, R. S. 68.
Hancox, D. 41.
Harmsworth, J. 51.
Harris fam. 57.
Hautinge. 22.
Hempton, Highway. 42.
    Spellings. 7.
Henry III. 16.
    IV. 9, 10.
    V. 9.
    VII. 9.
    VIII. 48.
Heythrop. 70.
Hirons, J. S. 43.
Hirons, W. 43, 62, 64.
Hodges, Dr. G. M. 78.
Holy Trinity, Guild of. 20.
Hudson, W. 43.
Hughes, Rev. J. 27, 55.

INDEX.

Ilbury Camp. 6.

Jhesus Scole. 50.
John, King. 10.
Jones, Dr. G. H. 26, 34, 78.
Jones, George. 73, 78.

Kempster. 16, 21, 51.
Kinch. 49, 77.
King's Sutton. 42.
Knibbs, J. 41, 77.

Lane, Dr. J. 53.
Lardner, Thos. 42.
Leaden Porch. 35, 58.
Lee-Dillon fam. 47.
Levellers. 76.
Long, H. 32.

Makepeace, Ann. 53.
Makepeace, Thos. 57, 65.
Malet, Walter. 11.
Manchip, T. A. 17, 51.
Mason, J. and S. 39.
Miller, The Misses. 34.
Mullis, E. 29.
Mummers. 71.

Neuport, William de. 13, 17.
Neuton, Hugh de. 17.
New College. 10, 24.
Newman, J. H. 55.
North fam. 47.
North Aston. 58, 69.
Nuthall, E. 27.
Nutt fam. 26, 53.

Odo, (Bishop of Bayeux). 7.
Owen, Nicholas. 32.

Parker, Rev. O. 33.
Pavilion. 73.
Perpount, Peter. 13.
Plot, Dr. 11, 70.
Pope, Sir Thomas and fam.
   10, 19, 32, 35, 46, 50, 57.
Port-Way. 70.
Pudding Pie Fair. 62.

Quintain. 70.

Rayer, T. 22.
Richard II. 10.
Risley, Rev. W. Cotton. 27, 33, 74.
Robertus, Dadyngton de. 9.

Scroggs, J. 44.
Scroggs, Sir Wm. 48.
Shutford. 42.
Simpson. 31, 58.
Skelton. 30.
Smith, J. H. 54.
Smith (Fiddler). 72.
Sonnibank, Dr. 27.
Stampe, John. 35.
Stilgoe, A. 37.
   H. E. 25, 37.
   Nathaniel. 25.
   Richard. 13.
   Family History. 58.
   Zachariah. 28, 32, 43.
Stonore, John de. 18.
Stratton (Croughton). 74.
Swere. 6.
Swift (Dean). 49.

Tchure. 33.
Trading Tokens. 53.
Trinity College, Oxford. 32, 35, 47.
Tucker, R. 39, 73.
Turner fam. 38, 78.

Valence, Ethelmar de, 16.

Walpole's British Traveller. 38.
Ward, J. 39.
Weaver, B. 65.
Wells (Puritan Divine). 15.
Wells & Son. 43.
Wheate, J. 23.
Wilkins, J. 19, 77.
William, Conqueror. 7.
Wilson. 27.
Wing, W. 29.
Windsor. 9, 58.
Woodhull, Nicholas. 33.
Woodstock. 36.
Wyer, J. and H. 23.
Wroxton. 17, 47.

UPDATING LOVEDAY

Miss H Loveday reported 80 species of birds, a formidable representation, from blackbird to woodcock, in her 'List of Birds in the District' (1933). Two species on this list, kittiwake and turtledove, do not appear in the Deddington Bird Group (DBG) list of 113 species of birds seen in 2007 (see W L Meagher, *Birds of Deddington Parish*, 2007). The greatest difference between the two lists is in the coverage given to the floodplain meadows of Clifton. To name a few from that habitat—the riverside and floodplain meadows of the River Cherwell—Canada goose, coot, common tern, herring gull, mute swan, pintail and tufted ducks are missing from her list. Of raptors, there is also a contrast. Loveday and DBG share kestrel and sparrowhawk.

The buzzard, seen by 11 of 21 observers in the DBG survey of 2007, was not seen by Miss Loveday, and she was surely right as the buzzard had not then come east from western woods (Gloucestershire, for example). Only in the last several years has the red kite been seen, and now more frequently, in Deddington; in Miss Loveday's era, the red kite had not yet been reintroduced to England. In all, the DBG recorded seven species of raptors to her two. Of owls, Loveday records 'barn, brown and little'; if 'brown' means tawny owl, then our lists agree.

Let me conclude with a short list of surprises—birds we see that she did not record: lapwing, nightjar, rook and skylark.

Common names of birds, as of plants, change, not only from time to time but also from place to place. 'Robin redbreast' has an affectionate tone; 'robin' is the new short form. 'Dabchick' is 'little grebe'; 'yellow hammer' is now one word; 'tree pippet' is 'tree pippit'. Finally, 'gold-crested wren' is 'goldcrest', a bird more often seen in the churchyard of St Peter and St Paul—where there are conifer trees—than elsewhere in the parish.

Walter L Meagher, September 2008